HANDBOOK

of

POLITICAL "ISMS"

HANDBOOK

of

POLITICAL "ISMS"

by

LOUIS WASSERMAN

Essay Index Reprint Series

BOOKS FOR LIBRARIES PRESS
FREEPORT, NEW YORK

In heaven there is laid up a pattern of it, methinks, which he who desires may behold, and beholding, may set his own house in order.

PLATO

Foreword

THIS book is an attempt to perform a simple educational service: to describe in objective terms the main elements of those competing social philosophies which are at grips in the world today. It is addressed to the men and women who value knowledge as a guide to action—in particular to those who may have labored earnestly for or against some "cause" whose meaning they neglected to search out beforehand.

The reader will be quick to recognize the limited scope of this volume. It is a dictionary of ideologies, each defined in terms of the principles and aims it professes for itself. The author has purposely denied himself the luxury of personal judgments. There is no attempt here to reconcile the ideal with the reality in operation. That is left to the many competent analyses that have appeared in recent years—some of which are included in the reading list given at the end of the book. A dictionary claims only to define, not to interpret; and, although definition leaves many gaps to be filled, no mature judgment is possible without a knowledge of what is to be judged.

The author cheerfully grants at the outset that complete objectivity is probably unattainable and that no brief statement of a comprehensive social theory can be adequate, particularly when some disagreement exists even among its partisans; but, after all this is granted, there still remains an acute need for a concise, factual, nonpartisan survey.

Social doctrines of the kind described here, whatever one may think of them, owe their origins not to the abstract theorizing of men nor to a troublesome preoccupation with utopias. In every case they represent a normal response of human beings to the conditions in which they live, to the shortcomings of their institutions, and to their conception of how the good life may be achieved. Every such doctrine has its historical setting; it proposes either to conserve all or part of what is, or to move into new forms that deliberately depart from those which exist. When a new social system triumphs, it is because the old lacked the ability to adapt itself to conditions which demanded change. It is only in such a circumstance that alternative systems have any chance of success. The rapidity of social change in recent years—either by adaptation or revolution—is directly linked to the unusual complexities of existence in modern society.

The author is indebted to the following persons for their criticisms of the original draft of this manuscript: Drs. Hugh Miller and Lewis Maverick of the University of California, Los Angeles; Dr. George Hedley, director, Pacific Coast School for Workers; Reverend Ernest Caldecott, First Unitarian Church, Los Angeles; Reverend and Mrs. Robert Whitaker, Los Gatos, California; and Dr. Robert R. R. Brooks of Williams College, for valuable suggestions on the final draft. To my wife, Caroline Leland Wasserman, I owe the constant encouragement and assistance that could have come from no other. For whatever shortcomings are evident, the author alone accepts blame.

Louis Wasserman

Contents

To What Degree Shall the Economy Be Collectively Owned?

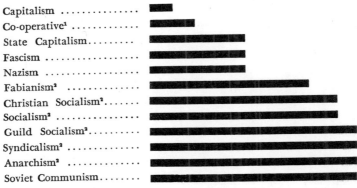

Capitalism ....
Co-operative[1] ....
State Capitalism.........
Fascism ....
Nazism ....
Fabianism[2] ....
Christian Socialism[2].......
Socialism[2] ....
Guild Socialism[2].........
Syndicalism[2] ....
Anarchism[2] ....
Soviet Communism........

[1] Emphasizes voluntary, small-group ownership operating on profit-sharing basis, as the alternative to privately-owned, profit-motivated enterprise.

[2] Emphasizes the creation of voluntary, self-governing producers' associations wherever feasible.

11

Proposed Methods of Change

CAPITALISM*—Minimum change; preserve *status quo* in property relations; function of government is to protect property, maintain order, enforce contracts, and permit economic processes to find own level of prices, production, income, and investment.

STATE CAPITALISM*—State professes satisfaction with private enterprise economy, but assumes the right to regulate, adjust, and modify economic processes for purposes of "general welfare."

ITALIAN FASCISM*—State permits operation of private enterprise, but under strict requirements of political expediency; production, prices, wages, profits, and capital investment controlled in greater or lesser degree; foreign trade a state function.

NAZISM*—Similar to *Italian Fascism.*

CO-OPERATIVE—Seeks to supplant private enterprise increasingly by extending scope of co-operative activities in distribution, processing, and production; concerned with economic action only; success is dependent upon establishing superiority of co-operatives in competition with private business.

ANARCHISM (Philosophical)—Condemns injustices of

* Names starred indicate those doctrines pledged to maintain essential form of private-enterprise economy; others aim to substitute alternate economic structure.

12

capitalistic society and seeks transition to a communal form, but advocates change commensurate only with religious convictions; nonviolent in character; personal, unorganized; "conversion by example."

FABIANISM—Propaganda, reform legislation, political methods; attempts to demonstrate superiority of public ownership, gradually, without disruptive change; compensation for property acquired by state.

SOCIALISM—Development of strong trade-union movement, political party to further program of transition, reform legislation, encouragement of co-operatives, propaganda; nonviolent change; compensation for property acquired.

CHRISTIAN SOCIALISM—Same as *Socialism;* change is believed to be justified on basis of fulfilling Christian principles.

GUILD SOCIALISM—Militant industrial-union activity in acquiring increasing control of economic processes; pressure exerted on state to acquire production properties, with compensation allowed; forcible change to be avoided if possible.

SYNDICALISM—Militant economic action, centered in industrial-union activity—boycott, sabotage, strikes, culminating in general strike; revolutionary action foreseen; political methods ignored.

ANARCHISM (Communist)—Same as *Syndicalism.*

COMMUNISM—Fulfillment of Marxian doctrine of the

"class struggle"; seeks transition to socialist society through abolition of *Capitalism;* methods include propaganda, militant trade-union activity, a political party devoted to Marxian principles, reform legislation; but each of these is considered preparatory to an unavoidable revolutionary uprising to terminate the capitalist state and its economy.

CHAPTER I

Democracy

I N ITS fullest sense, democracy is a social philosophy governing the whole of human relations, personal and collective. It is dynamic in character and sensitive to changing demands. Democracy must not be thought of as a completed pattern of society, of government, or of an economic system. It does not become static at any point of its development. The institutions it brings into being are tentative and flexible, and are likely to differ among different peoples at different stages.

The description of democracy that follows is not a portrait of the United States or of any other "democratic" country. It is rather a statement of the principles, assumptions, and implications underlying democracy as a social philosophy. To the extent that the social relations and institutions of a state are guided by that philosophy, it may be said to be democratic.

RESPECT FOR PERSONALITY

The key to an understanding of democracy is to be found in its deep respect for human personality—a respect that is extended impartially to every member of society, without regard for birth, wealth, or social position. The best statement of this attitude is to be found in the Declaration of Independence: "that all

men are created equal; that they are endowed by their
Creator with certain unalienable rights; that among
these are life, liberty, and the pursuit of happiness."
Democracy sets out to guarantee to each individual the
full realization of his capacities in whatever degree, great
or small, he may be endowed.

EQUALITY OF STATUS

Because the majority of the people under the historic
conditions of class privilege have been denied this basic
right, democracy insists that the position of men in
society must rest on a basis of essential equality.   Any
form of discrimination that would subject some individuals to an inferior or unequal status is considered a
violation of the democratic spirit.   Each person is to be
regarded as a worthy end in himself, not as a means to
other ends.   To all men is granted the right of self-
realization, but to none the privilege of exploiting or
obstructing others.

The principle of equal opportunity does not, of
course, presume equal development for all; the levels of
attainment naturally depend upon individual capacities.   But in this principle is discovered one of democracy's unique contributions: it conceded for the first
time the equal right of self-realization to all the people,
instead of limiting this right to those who by inherited
or acquired power could dominate the others.   The
implications of this principle give the prevailing tone to
the character of the state, the economic system, and the
social institutions of democratic society.

DEMOCRATIC INSTITUTIONS

Social institutions in a democracy are motivated by a single function: to equip each individual with advantages drawn from collective relationships. The value of political, economic, and cultural institutions is measured by their service to the prevailing democratic aim: equal opportunity for all in realizing the good life.

PERSONAL FREEDOM

First of all, in what may be considered a negative aspect, democratic society is pledged to protect the individual against violation of his personal liberty—to preserve at all times his freedom of choice and action. To this end, each person is declared equal before the law, each is granted an equal voice in the determination of public policy, and each is protected in his expression by the exercise of civil liberties. But, beyond this, it is the more positive duty of society to create new opportunities for self-development, encourage scientific research, extend educational training, establish a high level of material welfare, and utilize the national resources for the benefit of all.

POLITICAL DEMOCRACY

The government of a democracy is at the same time the servant of the people, the guarantor of their liberties, and the agency for the advancement of public ends. And since no single person or self-appointed class can be trusted to interpret the welfare of all, democracy lodges the power of sovereignty (political control) with the whole people. Public policy arises as the expression of

The Government of the United States

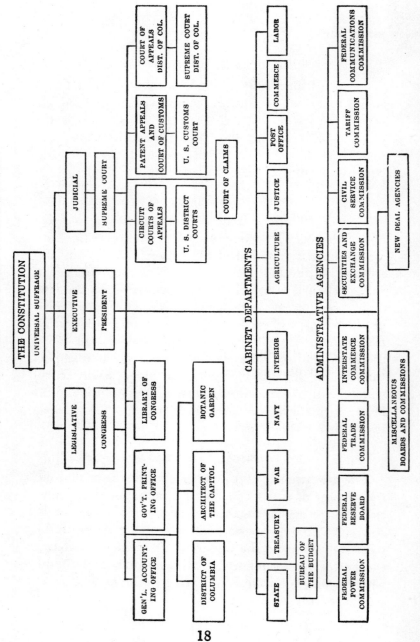

THE CONSTITUTION
UNIVERSAL SUFFRAGE

LEGISLATIVE   EXECUTIVE   JUDICIAL

CONGRESS   PRESIDENT   SUPREME COURT

GEN'L. ACCOUNTING OFFICE   GOV'T. PRINTING OFFICE   LIBRARY OF CONGRESS

DISTRICT OF COLUMBIA   ARCHITECT OF THE CAPITOL   BOTANIC GARDEN

CIRCUIT COURTS OF APPEALS   PATENT APPEALS AND COURT OF CUSTOMS   COURT OF APPEALS DIST. OF COL.

U. S. DISTRICT COURTS   U. S. CUSTOMS COURT   SUPREME COURT DIST. OF COL.

COURT OF CLAIMS

CABINET DEPARTMENTS

STATE   TREASURY   WAR   NAVY   INTERIOR   AGRICULTURE   JUSTICE   POST OFFICE   COMMERCE   LABOR

ADMINISTRATIVE AGENCIES

BUREAU OF THE BUDGET

FEDERAL POWER COMMISSION   FEDERAL RESERVE BOARD   FEDERAL TRADE COMMISSION   INTERSTATE COMMERCE COMMISSION   SECURITIES AND EXCHANGE COMMISSION   CIVIL SERVICE COMMISSION   TARIFF COMMISSION   FEDERAL COMMUNICATIONS COMMISSION

MISCELLANEOUS BOARDS AND COMMISSIONS   NEW DEAL AGENCIES

18

the common will: each person is to have an equal voice in its determination, with the decision of the majority translated into law. Democratic control is exercised through universal suffrage and the active participation of those who are governed. A complex social system requires that the people rule indirectly through elected representatives, who are pledged to carry the people's program into effect. The government is to be kept sensitive at all times to the changing needs of the people; required reform can then follow in an orderly way. If mistaken action should prevail for a time, the presumption is that it will be recognized and corrected.

The practical application of democracy to government has given rise to a large assortment of political techniques. These differ widely among the several nations utilizing the democratic philosophy, but all are intended to make the government increasingly responsive to popular control. Some of the most prominent of these instruments are: a constitution, embodying fundamental rights; separation of powers among the executive, legislative, and judicial branches; the "check and balance" system; regular elections; the secret ballot; proportional representation; opposition political parties; the right to recall elected officials; and the initiative and referendum. A republican form of government is probably the type of structure most conducive to political democracy. But there are enough exceptions: the kingdom of Sweden, for example, is recognized as far more democratic than the republic of Turkey. What is important is the substance of democratically inspired institutions, not their form.

CIVIL LIBERTIES

Doubtless one of the critical factors both in the self-development of the individual and the maintenance of popular control is the free expression of the people in all matters that concern their welfare. For this reason, the civil liberties—freedom of speech, press, assembly, of religious worship, and the right of petition—are to be guaranteed to all; and the active participation of every adult in public affairs is not only a privilege but a duty. A well-informed electorate is to be encouraged, through free discussion of social problems and the presentation of opposed points of view. The conviction here is that differences of opinion are a healthy influence, and that out of the conflict of ideas there is likely to emerge a sounder conclusion. Where the "rule of reason" prevails, the majority decision should reflect the most desirable action. Coercion of minority groups by force, or by denying them freedom of expression, violates the democratic spirit. The method of democracy is rather to rely on the judgment of a well-informed citizenry. The minority is free to become the majority if it can win enough adherents to its cause. In the words of the late Justice Holmes: "The best test of truth is its ability to gain acceptance in the market-place of ideas."

FAITH IN EDUCATION

Closely related to the principle of an intelligent electorate is the deep-lying democratic faith in universal free education. Enlightened mass decisions are clearly impossible without widespread educational oppor-

tunity.   But beyond this, the goal of democracy—full
self-realization for all—demands continuing access to
vocational and cultural advancement.   Education must
be universal, free, and objective.   The claims of every
field of knowledge are to be given consideration, controversial issues freely discussed. and teachers unham-
pered by external pressures.   The findings of science,
whatever their effect upon prevailing beliefs, are to be
permitted full expression.

DEMOCRACY AND CAPITALISM

Democratic theory specifies no particular form of
economy, simply providing in respect of this (as of other
institutions) that its operations be conducted not as
ends in themselves but as means of advancing individual
and collective welfare.   To the extent that it serves this
purpose, the economic system, whatever its form, is consistent with the larger aims of democracy.

It is worth noting here that modern capitalism arose
side by side with the movement for political democracy,
both movements representing a reaction against the
feudal autocracy of the Middle Ages.   In both fields
the reaction took the shape of a *laissez-faire* ("let-alone")
policy, designed to minimize the interference of autocratic governments with individual liberty.   As a result,
capitalism and political democracy became closely
identified, with the doctrine of individualism the key-
note of both.   But with the appearance of large-scale
industry in the nineteenth century, economic individualism came into increasing conflict with the principles
of social and political equality.   At the same time, the

extension of the suffrage to larger sections of the population furnished an instrument for reshaping democratic aims in the economic field. As a consequence, the political state has intervened increasingly by way of regulation and public ownership to subordinate individual enterprise to the collective welfare.

It may be said that, in the first phase of development, democratic peoples freed themselves from the autocratic state; in the second, having attained popular control, they are engaged in shaping the democratic state to their will. No institution is acknowledged as final, whatever its existing form; but any change in its character must be sanctioned by majority action. A capitalistic economy would remain consistent with democracy as long as it contributed a maximum of material welfare and did not violate the superior requirements of personal and social progress. Otherwise, a proper observance of democracy would require that capitalism be altered to the extent necessary to fulfill these conditions.

HISTORICAL ORIGINS

Democracy as an organized movement can be understood only with reference to its historical background. The early Greek city-states are commonly credited with the first observance of democracy, but theirs was at best a limited affair, in part nullified by the practice of slaveholding. The Middle Ages provided some examples of democratic theorizing, and the medieval church preached the spiritual brotherhood of man. But, as a modern movement, democracy may be said to have come into being in the sixteenth century, almost simultaneously in three fields. In the religious, it was the Protestant Reformation, seeking to establish the right of private conscience; in the political, it was the revolt of oppressed peoples against their autocratic rulers; and in the economic, the rise of the new commercial class in opposition to the landowning aristocracy. Where there had been too much authority before, the pendulum swung to the opposite extreme: private judgment in religion, liberalism in politics, and *laissez-faire* in business.

The next two centuries saw the conflict intensified in a series of revolutions, notably in England, Holland, France, and the United States, with democratic principles rapidly spreading to all civilized nations. Since then, the exponents of democracy have been concerned with the adaptation of their philosophy to immediate political and economic problems. The result has been the broadening of the franchise, the development of representative government, and the pouring of a complete set of political techniques into the parliamentary mold.

CHAPTER II

Liberalism

LIBERALISM is the movement, reflected both in a *spirit* and in a *body of doctrine,* that is dedicated to the expression of personal freedom in every sphere of life. This twofold character of liberalism—first as a general social outlook and next as an adherence to certain accepted institutions—is at the bottom of the sharp disagreement between liberal groups today. Both interpretations can be understood only in their historical setting.

HISTORICAL ORIGINS

In common with other social movements liberalism came into being not as a set of abstract ideals but as an expression of the material interests of men set in the framework of a particular time and place. The time was, roughly, the sixteenth century; the place, western Europe. The circumstances were such as to compel the emergence of a new philosophy that would reflect the revolutionary changes then in process of reshaping the physical world. In a measure liberalism preceded, later accompanied, and finally crystallized these external changes.

The liberal spirit first appeared as the revolutionary instrument of the newly emerging "middle class" in its struggle against the medieval church and state. Feudal society had everywhere been characterized by despotism, privilege, and rigid class lines. In the political field absolute monarchy prevailed, modified only by the equal oppression of nobility and clergy; the majority of the people possessed neither political power nor the means of obtaining it. In the economic field the land-holding aristocracy exercised effective control; royal monopoly flourished; the basis of wealth was land rather than liquid capital; production was jealously limited by the craft guilds; the lending of money at interest was frowned upon; and the entire conduct of business was bound up in a net of ecclesiastical restrictions designed to hamper initiative and discourage the accumulation of wealth. The medieval church was itself the largest landholder in Europe; in its combined spiritual and temporal role it penetrated into every fold of the social fabric, compelling even the homage of kings. This was the society against which the liberal movement was launched. It was upon the newly emerging middle class of traders, manufacturers, and bankers that the burden of economic oppression fell most heavily and with which the rise of liberalism is inescapably connected.

THE LIBERAL APPROACH

The principles of liberalism were embedded in the ideal of individual freedom; their goal was the emancipation of men from every form of external restraint. The character of the old society had been static, repressive, intolerant of change; the character of the new was typically free, dynamic, antitraditional. Liberalism claimed for all men the exercise of certain "natural rights," eternally secured to the individual and beyond the province of any political authority. Among these the most essential were freedom of inquiry, of expression, of religious conviction, of association, and of action. Through their exercise, it was believed, men could assert themselves most effectively, could realize their fullest capacities, and thus find their proper level in the social scheme.

The liberal spirit was pervaded throughout with an attitude of tolerance and reason, as opposed to force and dogma. It denied the right of discrimination or privilege in any form. It expressed an unbounded faith in social progress and in the possibilities for human betterment. It affirmed that social institutions have but one purpose—to serve, not to oppress—and that when any institution became subversive of that end it was the right of the people to alter or replace it with a new one.

ECONOMIC LIBERALISM

The movement to liberate the ingenuity and productive forces of man from the shackles of his feudal economy represented the first organized offensive of the liberal movement. In the economic field individual liberty meant the freedom to organize business, produce goods without limit, negotiate contracts, carry on trade, seek unrestricted profits, and exploit productive resources without state interference. The formula for this system, classically expressed by Adam Smith in his *Wealth of Nations,* was that of *laissez-faire*—the doctrine which, relying upon the notion of natural harmony, declared that if economic laws were allowed to operate

unchecked the result would be maximum productivity
and well-distributed wealth. The basic requirement
was the right of free enterprise. Granted this condition,
each individual in being spurred to his maximum efforts
by the prospect of material gain would automatically
harmonize his interests with those of the whole society,
and in the same automatic way the forces of supply and
demand would regulate the production, price, and purchase of goods. Conversely, any attempt by the state
or by combinations of either employers or employees to
modify the free play of competitive forces would only
cause obstruction and loss for all concerned. Based
upon this principle, liberalism in the economic field
became the doctrine of modern capitalism.

POLITICAL LIBERALISM

In its early period, liberalism's conception of the
state (as a reaction from feudal autocracy) was largely
negative and entailed the curtailment of political power
to a minimum. Only by this check, it was believed,
could individual freedom be assured. By the eighteenth
century, however, a new attitude had grown up: liberals
observed that freedom could be assured only when liberal principles were written into the law. Political liberalism in succeeding years, therefore, came to be
expressed in positive political action: the drafting of
constitutions and bills of rights; the growth of representative government; the broad extension of suffrage;
systems of checks and balances; codification of public
law; and similar measures. Ultimate sovereignty was

held to reside in the people as a whole, and political institutions were to be kept sensitive to the popular will.

OPPOSED INTERPRETATIONS

Liberalism thus fostered two broad tendencies that were to come into direct conflict: economic individualism and political collectivism. When free enterprise, intent on profit-making, began to produce less natural harmony than severe discords, popular control set itself to exert restrictions upon economic freedom. The result was the development of the "social-service" state of the late nineteenth century. Liberals chose to lean heavily upon political methods to preserve their aims in other areas. Capitalism was to be reformed, but not abolished. Wherever necessary the political state would intervene to guarantee freedom, check monopolistic practices, provide minimum standards for the conduct of industry, permit the organization of trade unions, and in general seek to mitigate the conditions of social inequality.

Two main schools of liberals may be distinguished in America today. The first insists upon the preservation of capitalist enterprise as essential to a free society and is prepared to support such a program of economic reform as mentioned above.

The second school of liberals places primary emphasis upon liberalism in its original character of *spirit* or *method* and refuses to accept capitalism as a necessary institution. They maintain that nineteenth-century liberalism has lost its earlier momentum and become hardened into a new set of privileges; that the freedom

it proclaimed in universal terms has become narrowed
by the owners of capital to permit exploitation of the
nonowners; and that political equality is mere empti-
ness unless accompanied by economic equality—in short,
that capitalist liberalism has come to threaten the very
existence of that democracy with which it was once in
harmony.

The new school of liberals therefore calls for an inter-
pretation of freedom based upon the relationships of
modern industrial society. The privilege of wealth
must be destroyed, so that human liberty will not be
subject to economic oppression. Moreover, the freedom of the individual must be set in the context of the
collective welfare. Specific liberties are not enough, it
is believed, until there is first a clear definition of the
purposes to which society is devoted. And, since the
possession of economic power is held to be the source
of political and social control, it is necessary in a society
where freedom is to be effective that the principal economic agencies be vested in the people as a whole rather
than left in the hands of profit-seeking individuals. Such
a change, it is believed, is consistent with liberal aims
and can be ushered in by liberal methods. In this inter-
pretation, liberalism becomes the advocate of evolutionary socialism.

LIBERALISM AND DEMOCRACY

The form of social organization which most nearly
incorporates the liberal attitude today is that of democracy—and, in fact, the two terms are often used interchangeably. In a precise sense, however, liberalism is a

habit of thought, to which democracy has given organizational content.

The liberal is in the position of a social scientist who examines human behavior in its historical context. He is devoted to a single ideal—that of human freedom—and he states the conditions under which that ideal can operate in the complex of society. It remains for organized social systems to grant this principle of freedom a greater or lesser place in their hierarchy of values. At the one extreme, anarchism exalts individual liberty above all else; at the other, Fascism submerges it completely in the state.

Democracy stands at a midway point, with personal freedom limited only by another concept—that of equality. It is here that the departure from liberalism really takes place. In the interests of equal status for all, which it considers basic to self-expression, democracy restricts the freedom of individuals wherever that freedom is found to be contrary to the collective good.

CHAPTER III

Capitalism

C APITALISM is the form of economy that depends for its operation upon the right of private enterprisers to engage freely in the search for profits under competitive conditions. It represents, to put it otherwise, the traditional striving for wealth, crystallized in a set of institutions whose character has now become clearly defined.

ECONOMIC INDIVIDUALISM

The justification of capitalistic enterprise is to be found in the doctrine of individualism applied to the sphere of economics. It is argued that the well-being of all society is best served when individuals are permitted the widest possible freedom of action. In the classical formulation of Adam Smith, a natural harmony of economic laws so operates as to achieve the welfare of all when each individual strives to acquire personal gain. With the prospect of unlimited profits as their reward, enterprisers and workers alike would exercise their highest skills to create a maximum of wealth; and this would necessarily mean the production of more and better goods for all. Business enterprisers would be guided in their production by the barometer of a free market, in which the demands of a multitude of consumers would indicate what needs existed to be satisfied.

31

It followed naturally from this that the role of government was to be reduced to a minimum in the economic field. Any interference with the natural processes of wealth production would merely diminish the amount of wealth produced. The function of the state should be to maintain order, protect property rights, enforce contracts, and guard against external invasion. It is entitled to operate in the sphere of education or to plan the construction of public works, but at no time to substitute public enterprise for that of private. The state might act as umpire, but never as participant, in the game of wealth production.

From this general outlook of economic individualism there have evolved the practical institutions of capitalism. Chief among these are the right to hold private property, freedom to engage in enterprise, profit-making as the incentive to production, the force of competition as automatic regulator, freedom of contract, the wage system, an intricate mechanism of exchange, and a policy of "rationalism" (systematic efficiency) in the conduct of business. A brief statement of each of these elements follows.

PRIVATE PROPERTY

The right of an individual to own property is assured by law in every form of existing society. But private property is of two main kinds: (1) goods for direct use by consumers in satisfaction of their wants, such as a house, an automobile, or a washing machine; and (2) capital goods, such as machinery, industrial plants, mines, raw materials, usable land, that are employed to produce or make the things used by consumers. This latter form of property is commonly referred to as the means of production. The ownership of such agencies by private enterprisers is regarded as the foundation stone of capitalism. It should be noted that possession of such property clearly implies the right to employ it in any legal way, to withhold it from use, to transfer it to others, or to pass it on by inheritance. In contrast to this practice, it may be pointed out, alternative economic systems such as socialism approve of private property in consumers' goods but contend that the means of production should be owned by society as a whole.

FREEDOM OF ENTERPRISE

Ownership of the means of production under capitalism may rest with one individual or with a group. As enterprisers they are free to utilize their property to acquire profits in whatever field they may choose. In doing so, they must assume the risk of the loss of their investment as well as the prospect of unlimited gain. In conducting their business, enterprisers are at liberty to produce as much or as little as they wish, to determine the nature and sale price of their products, employ whatever personnel is necessary, and make whatever commitments may seem advisable for successful operation. Business relationships between buyer and seller, employer and employee, are everywhere marked by freedom of contract. Such obligations receive the enforcement of public law.

THE PROFIT MOTIVE

The mainspring of capitalistic enterprise is the expectation of private gain in a measure greater than that of a mere livelihood. Capitalism counts upon man's inherent desire for acquisition as the most powerful incentive to production. The enterpriser is expected to exert his utmost initiative and ingenuity if the prospects for gain are unlimited; he will thus constantly strive to improve his product, lower his costs, expand his market, and render the best service. In the measure that the enterpriser succeeds in this, he will be rewarded by profits. Production will be engaged in only if it promises financial success; a venture operating at a loss will soon be abandoned. The incentive of profit is regarded as the surest guarantee of successful enterprise.

COMPETITION

Competition is the device depended upon to act as the automatic regulator of capitalism. The interaction of competitive forces in a free market is expected to stabilize prices, profits, and costs of labor. Thus, the competition of the producers in a given field of enterprise would tend to reduce market prices, while the competition of consumers to purchase those goods would tend to raise prices to a point where the producers would be assured a profit. Similarly, the competition of workers for available jobs would tend to depress the scale of wages, while the bidding of employers for workers would result in raising wages. This ideal situation, of course, presumes adequate mobility of capital and labor, relatively equal bargaining power among the groups, and a free market unhindered by monopoly.

THE WAGE SYSTEM

The owners of capital assume the risks of enterprise and absorb whatever profits may be forthcoming. Labor is regarded, like machinery and materials, as an item of cost. Workers are employed at an agreed wage, which remains constant, no matter how the fortunes of the enterpriser may fluctuate. The scale of wages is determined by the employer, although this factor depends somewhat upon the availability of labor and the strength of collective bargaining of the employees.

With the growth of huge industrial enterprises, relations between employer and employee have become largely depersonalized. The effect has been to create a more or less clear-cut division between owners and workers. Since labor is essentially an element of cost to the capitalist, his normal inclination is to keep that cost at a minimum. The worker, on his part, seeks always to raise his standard of living; as a consequence, his loyalty is more likely to attach to his union than to his employer. At the same time, it is evident that the dependence of the worker on his job for his livelihood gives him a primary interest in the success of the enterprise.

EXCHANGE AND FINANCE

To facilitate the exchange of goods produced in large quantities and distributed over a wide area, capitalism has developed a highly flexible system of finance. The value of goods and services is measured in terms of price; for convenience, price is expressed in units of a money standard, commonly based on gold. In order to introduce even greater flexibility, paper instruments such as bank notes, personal checks, stock certificates, promissory notes, and mortgages are extensively used wherever speed, convenience, or large-scale transactions are involved. Spreading over all these is the structure of credit, an evidence of promise to pay in the future. Banks, investment companies, and stock exchanges are the clearing houses for this intricate network of finance whose operation at all times is extremely sensitive to change.

This entire procedure is by no means an exclusive feature of capitalism but must be included as an essential element.

RATIONALISM

Since the extraction of profits depends upon the use of successful business methods, there exists in capitalistic enterprise a continuing drive to increase productivity and decrease costs. This policy is known as "rationalism" and consists of applying the principles of scientific management to industry, of increasing business efficiency through co-ordination, of utilizing exact accounting practices, of creating a division of labor to result in maximum production per unit, of purchasing under the most favorable conditions, and of uncovering new markets wherever possible. Machine processes are substituted for human labor at every stage where it may

be advantageous. Output of goods is geared to the highest point of profitability, at whatever rate of actual production that may occur.

STAGES OF CAPITALIST DEVELOPMENT

Capitalism must not be thought of as a deliberately
planned system, consciously applied. It consists rather
of a faith, or expression of confidence, in the ability of
"natural laws" to translate a multitude of personal, unplanned economic desires into a maximum of social
satisfaction. Capitalistic enterprise simply reflects the
behavior of men, freed from every possible restraint,
engaged in the competitive struggle for private gain.
The elements of private enterprise, described briefly
above, have become the institutional response to that
behavior.

The beginnings of capitalism as a prevailing mode
of economic life may be traced to the thirteenth century. The notion of free enterprise sprang from the
opposition of the rising class of merchants and bankers
(the "bourgeoisie") to the binding restrictions of the
existing feudal economy.[1] By the sixteenth century
this protest became articulate with the rise of economic
liberalism, which confidently predicted social well-
being as a consequence of free business enterprise.

The industrial revolution of the eighteenth century
gave tremendous impetus to the growth of capitalism.
The invention of new power machinery made mass production possible. The market for raw materials and
finished goods became world-wide. Huge profits fur-

---

[1] See Chap. II for more detailed description of this point.

nished new capital for expansion. Vast industrial units displaced the small factories and workshops that previously had succeeded the domestic handicraft and guild systems; and independent artisans and craftsmen, unable to compete with machine technology, became dependent wage workers. An intricate system of finance evolved to handle the problems of mass production, and, as competition spread to an international scale, the struggle for colonial domination by the industrial nations took the world stage. This was the merchant, or expansionist, period of capitalism.

The outbreak of the First World War ushered in a new phase of capitalist development. Technological invention and scientific management had previously made possible new levels in the production and distribution of goods. But simultaneously the rate of expansion of enterprise has slowed down appreciably. Competition and the free market have been haltered through the formation of trade associations, combinations, trusts, and monopolies. There is a strong tendency toward the concentration of economic power as large corporate units increase their domination of industry. The role of finance takes on special importance in arranging mergers, consolidations, stock trusteeships, and transfers of ownership through investment shares.

At the same time, the strictly private character of business has been modified by increased governmental regulation and the rise of organized labor. As the recurring cycles of boom and depression affect the public welfare more and more vitally, the government intervenes to cushion the shocks of readjustment. The attempt is made through the medium of detailed legislation to make the conduct of enterprise more responsive to social considerations. Municipalities and other public agencies enter into the ownership of public utilities, side by side with private enterprise. The role of the state approaches that which it exercised at the beginning of the capitalist era, but under conditions of popular, rather than autocratic, control.

CAPITALISTIC SOCIETY

A final factor demands at least brief mention—the influence of capitalistic enterprise upon the cultural pattern of society. It is self-evident that the economic system, whatever its form, permeates almost every instance of human behavior—the standard of living, conditions of health, habits of food and dress, amusements, political outlook, social level, personal values. Behavior is unavoidably tied up with the amount of income earned and the relationship in which individuals stand to the economic system.

Capitalism, urged on by the dynamic of wealth acquisition, has left a profound imprint upon the character of social institutions wherever it exists. It is necessary only to observe the contrasting values claimed by alternative economic systems to appreciate this fact.

CHAPTER IV

State Capitalism
(State Socialism)

SINCE the late nineteenth century the governments of industrial nations have exhibited a strong tendency toward increased participation in economic affairs. This tendency is identified as state capitalism or, in a somewhat different sense, state socialism. The development is notable in that it marks an abandonment of the classical conception of enterprise as a strictly private matter and affirms the right of government to intervene for whatever purpose it may feel is required by the public welfare.

As such, the tendency toward state capitalism is to be found in all stages of maturity, from the mild version of the American "New Deal" to the totalitarian completeness of German and Italian Fascism. In each case the state has encroached upon the independence of a free economy to the point where governmental ownership, regulation, or control affects to a greater or lesser extent the decisions of producers and consumers.

REASONS FOR INCREASED INTERVENTION

Several factors have contributed to this tendency. In the first place, the economic processes of a state have always been affected by political and military needs; modern economic warfare has magnified the impor-

tance of this factor. Secondly, the government has been
increasingly called upon to cushion the shocks of cyclical
depressions; emergency controls, once installed, have
tended to remain. Thirdly, the growing influence of
organized labor has forced the state to assume responsibility for industrial relations, price and wage levels,
social insurance, re-employment, and the like. At the
same time, consumers' interests have demanded protec-
tion against predatory business practices. Finally, the
conviction has become widespread that government
should assume the ownership and operation of such
projects as private enterprise was unwilling or unable,
or could not be entrusted, to operate: postal services,
public roads, money control, water supply, regional
power developments, bridges, etc. Some impetus has
been furnished by the desire of government and business leaders to offset the insistent demands of socialists
for complete nationalization of the basic industries.

FEATURES OF STATE CAPITALISM

Nevertheless, a large part or most of industry remains
in private hands under state capitalism. Production is
carried on for profit; freedom of contract still prevails;
employers retain the right to hire and fire, and to
prescribe wages and working conditions—but within
limited scope. The state frequently owns and operates
banking and credit agencies, transport and communication, and certain natural resources. It may act as monop-
olist in certain fields, such as liquor or armaments,
either to safeguard the public interest or to raise revenue.
Often it will subsidize private business for purposes

that seem advisable or necessary, and again offer to "socialize" losses to encourage production. Through fiscal policies or the threat of competition, the government exerts a strong indirect influence on private producers.

The administrative functions of government are necessarily enlarged under state capitalism. Numerous agencies undertake to secure conformance to the law and to operate public enterprises. The attitude of the state may, in a word, be described as paternalistic. The government interposes its political authority in the attempt to reconcile economic individualism with the general welfare, to harmonize the conflicting demands of labor, capital, and the consumer—either in the role of arbiter or of master. There is a clear implication that in this process the freedom of individuals and of groups will be abridged to some extent.

No modern industrial nation has escaped the trend toward state capitalism. Especially since the First World War, government ownership and control of economic functions has been on the increase. With the onset of the world-wide depression in 1929, the private character of business may be said to have been definitely supplanted by collectivist considerations.

BY WHOM, FOR WHOM, AND TO WHAT ENDS?

The fact that state capitalism is a response to the development of certain economic forces falls far short of explaining its real nature. The crux of the problem lies in the answer to three questions:

1. By whom is the power of the state administered?
2. For whose benefit is collectivism undertaken?
3. To what ends is it directed?

Among the criteria involved in making adequate judgments on these issues would be the following:

1. Does the government rest on popular consent and are elected officials responsible to their constituents?
2. Is there effective freedom to criticize governmental policy and to initiate opposition?
3. Are the results of state operation and control clearly intended to benefit the whole population or just a segment?
4. Can labor express itself as an independent force, or does its welfare lie in the hands of employers and state?
5. Does any single economic group unduly influence governmental policy?
6. Finally, for what purpose does government intervene? Is it (1) with the primary object of preserving capitalism, (2) to pave the way to a new economic system, (3) to favor a particular economic class, or (4) to combine both political and economic power in few hands for more ulterior aims?

STATE SOCIALISM

The name "state socialism," when used interchangeably with state capitalism, is apt to be misleading. The term is properly applied to an economy in which the government has already largely secured control of basic industry, with the definite aim of complete nationalization.[1] But state socialism differs from orthodox socialism in that it is likely to be based on middle-class rather than working-class support, relies mainly upon political action to effect the transition, and does not contemplate

---

[1] As contemplated by Fabianism. See Chap. XI.

a radical revision of social values and institutions. For
these reasons Marxian socialists regard with deep dis-
trust the increase of state power unless the government
has been placed under working-class control and is
clearly aiming at ultimate socialism.

CHAPTER V

Marxism

MARXISM is the theory and program of revolutionary socialism. Its groundwork is an analysis of history which traces the origin of social institutions to economic forces. As political theory, Marxism is a description of the class structure of society, in which the political state appears as the ruling instrument of the dominant class. As economic theory, it is a critique of the capitalist mode of production, an explanation of how labor is exploited by the owners of capital, and of how this process must inevitably lead to industrial breakdown. As a revolutionary program, Marxism outlines the tactics of class struggle, leading to the overthrow of the capitalist state and the establishment of a socialist society.

The chief elements of Marxism, described briefly below, form the basis of the two major social doctrines: evolutionary socialism and revolutionary socialism (communism). The latter of these follows the Marxian analysis in all important details. The former, evolutionary (or gradualistic) socialism, stems from a "revised" Marxism, in which the theory of class conflict and the need for revolutionary action have been deleted. To the original doctrine formulated by Marx and Engels, Lenin later added an analysis of capitalism in the "im-

perialist" stage and clarified the tactics of revolutionary struggle.[1]

MATERIALIST INTERPRETATION OF HISTORY

Marx concerns himself first with a search for general
laws of historical development. Society, he concludes,
must be regarded as a dynamic process undergoing constant change, continuously experiencing the growth,
development, and decline of its forces. Throughout
this process there is a cause-and-effect relationship, so
that each phase of history in a given society necessarily
contains the principal elements of the preceding phase,
and in turn furnishes the soil out of which the succeeding phase will grow.

Historical development springs from the interaction
of men with the material conditions in which they live.
Human capacities, mental and physical, are combined
with the resources of the natural environment, in the
endeavor to provide goods and services usable for mankind. There arises of necessity a compatible form of
social organization through which the processes of production, distribution, exchange, and consumption may
operate. Upon this structure is erected in turn the
whole complex of human relationships, the institutions
of civilized society—legal, political, ethical, and cultural.

The character of the whole structure is conditioned
by its economic base. Social classes take shape in
response to their share and control of wealth produc-

---

[1] The terms "Leninism" and "Bolshevism" are used to describe the
application of Marxism to the transformation of Russia into the first
socialist society.

tion. The law is written to safeguard existing property
relationships, and the state reflects the will of the dominant economic group. Foreign policy is guided by
industrial wants. Even social morality is the subtle expression of materialist values. Moreover, the educational process provides the medium through which this
entire culture is transmitted and preserved. Marx implies no ethical judgment in thus describing these
phenomena, but records them as what he believes to be
observable fact. Other forces in history—the power of
ideals, great leaders, and the like—Marx does not deny;
but these, he contends, sprang from, and were conditioned by, the material factors of their environment,
then in turn reacted upon those conditions. The
essence of ideals, for example, is that they represent an
attempt to alter, or escape from, the realities that exist.

CLASS STRUGGLE

The processes of wealth production in any given
society, Marx continues, are in a state of constant altera-
tion as improved methods of technology are invented
and applied. It was thus, for example, that the small-
scale handicraft economy of the Middle Ages was forced
to give way before the factory system of machine production. Invariably new social relationships, taking
their cue from the revised property status, accompany
such changes. Economic classes are organized on the
basis of their participation in wealth production,
whether as slave or master in early times, or as owner,
investor, or wage earner in modern times. Each group
arises naturally as a result of the common status and

unity of interests among its members. Each class seeks
to obtain for itself a larger and larger proportion of
the total income produced, the dominant class arrayed
always against those who threaten their power and
property.

The struggle is only for a time confined to the economic field, then becomes transferred to the political
arena. Here the central fact in history, Marx asserts,
has been that the dominant economic class has brought
the political state under its own control, realizing that
only by this means could its economic power be consolidated. The state in its historic role is, therefore,
not an impartial body dispensing evenhanded justice,
but rather the product of class antagonisms in society,
the "executive" of the owning class.

Whereas the shifts in economic techniques and the
need for new relationships develop imperceptibly and
bring with them the demand for a transfer of control,
the outmoded economic class invariably refuses to surrender its political dominance to another. There follows an intensification of the struggle. The emerging
class, finding itself everywhere hampered by an outworn
social structure, is finally compelled to seize political
power by forcible means, erect a new state in sympathy
with the changed form of economy, and make legal the
new property relationships. The history of society, says
Marx, has been the history of such class struggles.

THEORY OF SURPLUS VALUE

In the era of capitalism, Marx continues, the class
alignments have become greatly simplified and the

issues of conflict much clearer. The essence of capitalism is the private ownership of the agencies of production by a relatively small class and the employment for
wages of the large mass of workers in society. Economic
relationships now group men increasingly into two
opposed classes, each motivated by a desire for an increased share in the social income: the capitalists (or
"upper bourgeoisie"), owners of the instruments of
production, who derive their income from rent, interest, and profits; and the "proletariat," the mass of skilled
and unskilled workers, who have no means of obtaining
a livelihood except by the sale of their labor power.
Under the system of law formulated in their own behalf,
the capitalists obtain a free hand in exploiting both the
natural resources of the nation and the working class
whom they employ. The method by which capital
exploits labor under capitalism is described by Marx
in the theory of "surplus value."

The eventual value of any commodity, he declares, is
measured by the amount of labor necessary to produce
it. (In this view, land is reckoned a passive agent, with
machinery, materials, and capital all derived from previ-
ous labor.) The workers who actually produce the
commodities, however, are paid not for their full share
of the production but only a minimum wage determined roughly by their subsistence requirements. The
capitalist sets the working day at a number of hours
that will return in market price of the goods not only
the amount of wages paid but a surplus fund as well.
This surplus is pocketed by the owners of capital in the
form of profits, rent, or interest. The worker, in other

words, produces more in market value than he is paid
for. This fact becomes reflected in a deficiency between
his income in wages and the value of the goods he has
produced for sale.

The resulting overbalance persists on the other side
as well, with the capitalists unable to consume normally
the total surplus they have acquired. The excess is
then expended on luxury goods (while needed production suffers), or diverted to new investments at home or
abroad. But this diversion, Marx claims, merely accen-
tuates the contradiction inherent in a capitalistic
economy: the tendency of production to increase while
the consuming power of the working population relatively decreases.

OVERPRODUCTION AND DEPRESSION

As a result, capitalism becomes subject, after its initial
stages of expansion, to a succession of deepening crises
of overproduction, balanced by conditions of increasing
misery for the workers. During its expansionist phase
capitalism can absorb these setbacks by exploiting new
markets, launching into the production of an ever
greater proportion of luxury goods, selling on credit
against the hope of future income, and reorganizing the
capital structure by intricate financing. With the
growing industrialization of backward nations, however, the erection of tariff barriers, and the drying up of
both foreign and domestic markets, capitalism enters
upon a period of decline from which it cannot, by the
very nature of its processes, recover. This final stage is
marked by the widespread displacement of workers by

machines, with consequent unemployment on a large
scale; an actual decrease in production for the home
market; the sacrifice of competitive enterprise to its
opposite, corporate monopoly; and an intensified
struggle for foreign markets and sources of investment
that culminates in wholesale warfare among the capitalistic powers.

The exploitation of the workers by the owners gives
rise to the class divisions of capitalist society. The ensuing conflict between the two classes, Marx affirms, is
not a policy deliberately planned by either but is unavoidably impelled by the situation itself.

PROGRESS OF THE REVOLUTIONARY STRUGGLE

Not only does capitalism contain the seeds of its own
destruction, says Marx, but it brings into being the class
that will eventually encompass its overthrow. That
class is the proletariat, the workers of hand and brain,
the real producers. As the number of capitalists decreases through the steady concentration of economic
control (the larger, more successful enterprises squeez-
ing out the smaller), the ranks of the proletariat will be
swelled by acquisition of the dispossessed.

As the effects of capitalist exploitation become more
evident, the class struggle intensifies. The proletariat
is educated to a consciousness of its mission in the overthrow of capitalism. The common plight of the workers
will engender first an instinctive group loyalty, then
active class consciousness. To this natural solidarity of
the masses will be added the militant guidance of a
group of trained leaders (the Communist Party), skilled

in an understanding of the economic processes and the tactics of social revolution. The struggle proceeds on every front—economic, political, intellectual. Workers are taught to organize; to bargain collectively for a greater share of income; to strike and boycott when necessary to win their demands; to build co-operative societies and form political parties devoted to these ends. Every tactic to dislodge capitalist control, gain concessions, and improve the lot of the working class is to be used in the struggle.

But concessions are not enough. The fight cannot ultimately be won until the control of the agencies of production has finally been wrested from the hands of private owners and the bourgeois state completely crushed. And here history has shown, says Marx, that no class ever surrendered its power and property without violent resistance. The workers must not be deluded by the vain hope that capitalism will consent to its own destruction. When finally threatened, it will use every agency at its command, the organs of propaganda, its huge wealth, the political state, and the armed forces, to keep itself in power. The workers must therefore be prepared for a final revolution, a mass uprising which will end in the extinction of the capitalist state.[2]

---

[2] It may be noted that Marx's insistence upon eventual armed insurrection did not preclude, either in his doctrine or his personal activities, collaboration with "bourgeois" allies whenever an immediate gain was in prospect. Thus, he engaged in the nineteenth-century struggles of parliamentarism against political autocracy. Present-day support by Marxists of New Deal reform measures is predicated on the same principle.

Although it is undeniable that Marxian doctrine is permeated throughout with the necessity of final revolt, the following passage, contained

SOCIALIST SOCIETY

The purpose of the overthrow of capitalism is to establish a socialist society, the foundation of which is to be the common ownership of the means of production and their operation for the general good. Class antagonisms, it is asserted, will be ended by the abolition of classes. There will no longer be owners and workers, but workers only. No individual or group will be permitted to live by the toil of others—that is, surplus value will be eliminated. Production will be organized on a planned basis, designed to eliminate competitive wastes and to supply a maximum of the needs wanted by consumers, without regard for profitability. Work will be available for everyone able to work; and, with economic security assured, there will be made possible a degree of individual freedom denied to the majority of workers under capitalism. The emphasis of socialist society will be placed upon co-operative living and collective responsibility.

PROLETARIAN DICTATORSHIP

During the period of reconstruction, however, Marx declares, the victorious workers must establish a dicta-

---

in a speech by Marx at the meeting of the First (Communist) International at Amsterdam in 1872, is often quoted as an offset:

But we do not assert that the way to reach this goal is the same everywhere. We know that the institutions, the manners, and the customs of the various countries must be considered; and we do not deny that there are countries like England and America, and, if I understood your arrangements better, I might even add Holland, where the worker may attain his object by peaceful means. But not in all countries is this the case.

torship to inaugurate their program and stamp out
counterrevolution. The period of this dictatorship is
indeterminate; it will last until a socialist economy is
firmly secured, until all vestiges of bourgeois society have
disappeared and the working class has grown to include
the whole people. Until that time, the proletarian
state is frankly a class dictatorship of the emancipated
workers over the opposition. When there are no longer
opposed classes, the state, whose historic function has
hitherto been that of class domination, will gradually
"wither away," leaving only a skeleton of administrative agencies. Socialist society is itself but the intermediate stage to usher in communism, the completely
classless, equalitarian society.

The historic progress of society from capitalism to
socialism to communism will differ in the time required
and in the circumstances under which each nation and
people find it possible to move from stage to stage. In
each country the process will follow the pattern of its
own social and cultural background, the extent of its
economic development, the degree of economic breakdown, the amount of acceptance of the Marxian program by the population, and the quality of the revolutionary leadership.

Marxism emphasizes the unity of working classes
throughout the world and urges the primacy of class
loyalty over that of any racial or national bond. The
victory of socialism, Marx declares, cannot be complete
until it shall encompass the workers of all the world.

CHAPTER VI

Socialism
(Evolutionary)

FROM the doctrine and program of Marxism are derived two major social movements: communism and socialism.[1] The first of these is generally accepted as completely orthodox—the application of revolutionary Marxian principles to contemporary society. As such, its elements will be dealt with in Chapter VII under the heading Soviet Communism.

The second, evolutionary socialism, is described below. Although resting on a Marxian base, it will be found to have undergone important modifications. The reality of class conflict is acknowledged, but its role is minimized. Revolutionary action has been replaced by gradualistic methods. Reimbursement for socialized property takes the place of outright confiscation. Furthermore, the political state is to be converted to democratic purposes, not destroyed, and the proposal of a transitional dictatorship is altogether rejected.

It will be helpful, first, to select from among the various uses of the term "socialism" the sense in which it shall be defined here. Socialism is not the same as social reform; it should not be confused with occasional public

---

[1] Elements of Marxism will also be found in such diverse doctrines as anarchism, syndicalism, guild socialism, Christian socialism, and Fabianism.

ownership; it does not refer to any particular brand of government; and in its present-day form it bears only the remotest relationship to past experiments in utopian or ideal societies. Despite the fact that socialists disagree in matters of detail no less than adherents of other doctrines, an acceptable outline of the movement in the United States can be readily sketched.

The main features of modern socialism may be summarized thus: (1) an attack on the prevailing mode of production and the distribution of income under capitalism, (2) a rough blueprint of the processes of a socialist economy, and (3) a plan of action to effect the transformation.

CAPITALISM CRITICIZED

The core of socialist doctrine is the requirement that the ownership and control of the primary means of production, distribution, and exchange shall be vested in the whole people, and operated by representative agencies to provide a maximum of economic well-being. In an ethical sense, socialism seeks to create a material environment most conducive to the growth of harmonious, constructive relationships among men.

It is precisely because socialists deny that such harmony is attainable within a profit-motivated society that they insist upon the transformation of the economic structure. The indictment leveled against capitalist enterprise is basically Marxian: that, whereas the ultimate source of all wealth is labor, a large portion of the wealth produced is intercepted by nonproducers through the instrumentality of rent or profits. The

consequences of this practice display a division of society
into opposed classes, extremes of poverty and wealth,
huge wastage of resources, the spread of corporate
monopoly, unemployment, and international warfare.
Ultimately, it is believed, this self-destructive process
can be brought to an end only by reclaiming for society
the ownership of its wealth-producing agencies. On the
issue of how the change may be accomplished, socialists
depart from orthodox Marxism in relying upon the
success of moderate, constitutional means.

CAPITALIST PRODUCTION

The socialist attack is directed fundamentally at the
practice of permitting wealth production to depend
upon the competitive struggle of individual enterprisers
motivated by profit. It is freely admitted that during
the pioneer stage of development the prospect of private gain was necessary to encourage the taking of risks,
and that the achievements of private enterprise in that
period were impressive. But socialists maintain that
since then the very processes inherent in capitalism have
raised up a complex of problems so grave as to threaten
the disruption of the whole social fabric.

Socialists oppose profit-making as the incentive of
enterprise, not on moral, but on economic grounds.
When production is geared to the rate of profit, the
result is often found to be restricted output at high
prices, rather than a plentiful supply at low prices. In
support of this contention the socialist points to the fact
of widespread underconsumption in the presence of idle
land, labor, and factories, and of the deliberate destruc-

tion of goods to maintain price levels. The roots of this
condition, he points out, lie in the grossly unequal distribution of income. The wage-earning population
receives too small a share to satisfy its needs, while the
owners of capital are enabled to live luxuriously, accu-
mulate larger surpluses, or divert their funds to foreign
investment. At the same time, technological improvements designed to reduce the prices of goods or increase
their length of service are frequently suppressed when
their release threatens the flow of profits. There exists
under capitalism, in short, a compulsion to scarcity because of the maldistribution of income inherent in profit-
making enterprise.

COMPETITION DISTORTED

Socialists furthermore deny that competition is either
beneficial or effective as the regulator of capitalist enterprise. On the one hand, it is claimed that competition
necessitates enormous wastes in production and distribution, much of it not only needless but harmful.
Moreover, it is found that the regulatory force of competition is rapidly being nullified by the invasion of corporate monopoly. Capital holdings have become increasingly concentrated in the hands of fewer and fewer
owners as smaller units fall by the wayside. Dominance
over the market by corporate monopoly makes the
hazards of business almost prohibitive to the small
enterpriser. In many fields, prices and production are
determined by agreement among major producers,
instead of being subject to the free interplay of supply
and demand. The actual ownership of industry, ac-

cording to socialists, has passed from the hands of enterprisers to those of financiers and investment trusts.
Business has become a "by-product of the activities of a
gambling casino."

INEVITABILITY OF BREAKDOWN

Nor is this self-destroying process to be considered a
mere perversion of legitimate enterprise.   On the contrary, socialists contend, all this is the logical outcome of
capitalist development.   From the first, its processes
have contained within themselves the seeds of their own
destruction.   So long as production must depend upon
a multitude of unplanned decisions, each motivated by
the urge to profit, the course of capitalist enterprise cannot be otherwise.   Piecemeal reforms, such as governmental intervention, control of the currency, social insurance, or even of increased wages for labor, can do no
more than deflect for a time the inevitable breakdown.

It is the socialist view that, in common with the outmoded economic systems of the past, capitalism must in
turn give way to an improved method of production
and distribution.   A transition to socialism is regarded
as the logical next step in economic evolution.   This
sense of the reasonableness of its demands underlies the
socialist conviction that the change can be made without serious disruption of existing institutions.

TRANSITION TO SOCIALISM

Departing from Marxian doctrine at this point, socialists refuse to concede that the parliamentary state must
necessarily be dominated by the property-owning class.

The modern state is regarded instead as having been brought under popular control by means of universal suffrage and the grant of civil liberties. The task remains to convert the state to a program of socialism through the conquest of public opinion.

Specifically, it is planned to use three main agencies. A socialist political party will organize citizens as voters to elect sympathetic officials and sponsor reform legislation. Workers will be organized in strong, class-conscious unions, preferably of the industrial type; their function will be not only to win immediate concessions but to furnish the nucleus for eventual self-government. Finally, consumers' co-operative societies will be fostered to promote the principles of nonprofit enterprise, improve the standard of living, and serve as "industrial commissaries" when strikes occur.

Socialism is essentially a working-class movement but believes, unlike communism, that it is possible to win the consent of the middle class to its program of change.

BUILDING THE SOCIALIST ECONOMY

The inauguration of a socialist economy is to proceed by successive stages within the framework of the existing state. The principal resources and industries of the nation will be acquired gradually from their private owners under the right of eminent domain. Compensation will be paid, presumably on the basis of the physical values of the property—payment taking the form of low-interest-bearing, nontransferable bonds, secured by operating revenue. Steeply graded income and inheritance taxes would be used to reduce excessive wealth and prevent new accumulations.

The order in which the means of production would be socialized contemplates early acquisition of such public utilities as light and power, the munitions industries, and the banking system; following that, the gradual absorption of such natural-resource properties as mining, lumbering, and petroleum, industries engaged in the manufacture of capital goods, and units of a monopolistic nature. Small-scale distribution, handicraft, and agriculture would remain at least temporarily unaffected by the process, although brought within the scope of national planning. Especially in these latter fields, cooperative societies for the production and marketing of goods would be encouraged.

ECONOMIC AGENCIES

The ownership and control of socialized properties would be lodged not with a single centralized government board but with a variety of public agencies—local, regional, and national. Thus, local communities would own and operate such ventures as gas and electric service, municipal bus lines, housing, health, and recreation; states or regional units would conduct mining, milling, or packing industries; and separate national agencies would be entrusted with such operations as a unified banking system, shipbuilding, transportation, and communication.

Over this whole structure of diversified ownership and management of enterprise would be established a permanent national planning board. The nature and volume of production would be gauged by the estimated needs of both consumers and producers; labor, machinery, materials, and technical ability would be allocated to each industry as required; the whole process would be co-ordinated by a balancing of the factors required to supply the needs of consumers and to replace and expand the means of production.

INCENTIVES UNDER SOCIALISM

Socialists refuse to concede the pre-eminence of profit-making as the incentive to efficient production. They point out, first, that the chance to acquire profits is restricted to a very small portion of the population—those who possess capital or the means of production. The overwhelming majority in a capitalist society, the wage earners, are motivated by the simple desire to earn a livelihood. For them, socialists claim, the opportunities would be even more favorable under a system in which their rewards would be proportionately greater. It is further maintained that while acquisitiveness is a common characteristic of human beings, its intensity has been unduly heightened under competitive capitalism. Devotion to the public service, desire for acclaim, sheer pleasure in accomplishment—these are cited as alternative motivations common among men of prominence at all times. Socialism contemplates a scale of wages, salaries, and bonuses for all types of services that is consistent with the formula: "from each according to his ability, to each according to his worth." Additional noneconomic rewards, such as public recognition, degrees, and special honors would be offered to encourage maximum effort.

DEMOCRACY UNDER SOCIALISM

With the establishment of "economic democracy" through collective ownership, socialists believe that the state will become more truly representative of the popular will than has ever been possible in capitalist society. Class divisions would no longer have a basis for existence. The corrupting effect of business interests on government would be removed. Through the exercise of popular suffrage, together with the right of recall and referendum, public opinion would be assured of direct control of both its political and economic representatives.

Similarly, with the exploitation of class by class removed, socialists foresee the creation of a social atmosphere marked by a degree of harmony greater than ever before realized. Coincident with the spread of socialism to other nations, it is believed that the major cause of war, imperialist rivalry for world markets, would be eliminated and a new order of peace ushered in for all mankind.

CHAPTER VII

Soviet Communism

OMMUNISM is organized Marxism in action. Its first distinction from evolutionary socialism lies in its method: Communists regard the class struggle as an inherent feature of capitalistic society, with the power of the state always at the service of the propertied class; the possibility of attaining socialism by way of gradual reform is abandoned, and communists direct their strategy toward an eventual seizure of power by armed force. The second distinction lies in the ultimate aim: In communist doctrine, socialism is itself but an intermediate phase, which must be consolidated under a workers' dictatorship—from which will finally emerge a society in which class divisions have been ended, the police power of the state abolished, and the harmony of individual and collective welfare achieved.

The successful application of communist theory and tactics has been responsible for transforming capitalistic Russia into the present-day Soviet Union.[1] It is this system of social, political, and economic organization

---

[1] "Soviet Union" is an accepted contraction of Union of Soviet Socialist Republics (USSR), the present official name of the territories formerly known as Russia. In the full name, the word "Union" signifies a voluntary alliance of sixteen (April, 1941) republics, acknowledging a common federal government; "Soviet" means simply a council of delegates for governing purposes, elected to represent constituencies of workers; "Socialist" identifies the economy as one in which common ownership of production goods prevails; the word "Republics" refers to the political subdivisions of the Union, which possess limited self-governing rights.

The Government of the Soviet Union

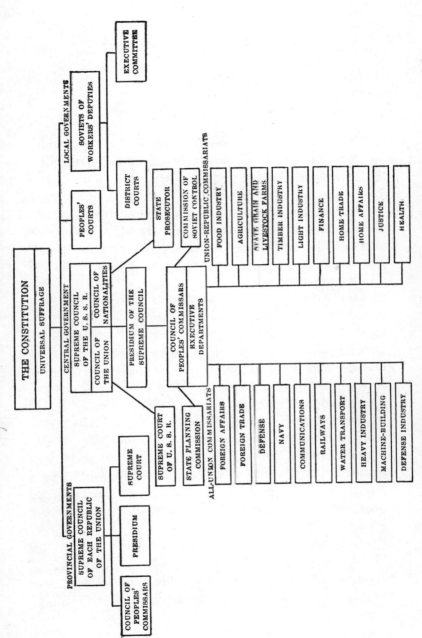

THE CONSTITUTION
UNIVERSAL SUFFRAGE

PROVINCIAL GOVERNMENTS
SUPREME COUNCIL OF EACH REPUBLIC OF THE UNION

COUNCIL OF PEOPLES' COMMISSARS

PRESIDIUM

SUPREME COURT

CENTRAL GOVERNMENT
SUPREME COUNCIL OF THE U. S. R.

COUNCIL OF THE UNION
COUNCIL OF NATIONALITIES

PRESIDIUM OF THE SUPREME COUNCIL

COUNCIL OF PEOPLES' COMMISSARS
EXECUTIVE DEPARTMENTS

SUPREME COURT OF U. S. R.
STATE PLANNING COMMISSION

LOCAL GOVERNMENTS
SOVIETS OF WORKERS' DEPUTIES
EXECUTIVE COMMITTEE

PEOPLES' COURTS
DISTRICT COURTS

STATE PROSECUTOR
COMMISSION OF SOVIET CONTROL

UNION-REPUBLIC COMMISSARIATS
FOOD INDUSTRY
AGRICULTURE
STATE GRAIN AND LIVESTOCK FARMS
TIMBER INDUSTRY
LIGHT INDUSTRY
FINANCE
HOME TRADE
HOME AFFAIRS
JUSTICE
HEALTH

ALL-UNION COMMISSARIATS
FOREIGN AFFAIRS
FOREIGN TRADE
DEFENSE
NAVY
COMMUNICATIONS
RAILWAYS
WATER TRANSPORT
HEAVY INDUSTRY
MACHINE-BUILDING
DEFENSE INDUSTRY

The Communist Party is not officially a part of the government, but dominates the political structure of the U.S.S.R. through a separate organization, which parallels the agencies of government.

65

that is described below under the title "Soviet Communism."

THE SOVIET STATE

The Soviet Union, having brought an end to its capitalist institutions is now, according to communists, in the transitional stage of socialism. This is evidenced by the fact that all but a negligible fraction of the land, properties, and resources of the nation are in public hands. The state is under the control of a proletarian dictatorship, administered by the Communist Party. No claim is made that the full goal of communism has yet been reached.

The Soviet State is a federal union of sixteen republics, with major political and economic functions exercised by the federal government. The individual republics possess self-governing institutions competent to legislate and administer their needs in fields not reserved to the state as a whole. The 1936 constitution of the USSR provides a political structure of soviets, or representative councils, rising like the levels of a pyramid from the 70,000 local soviets, through those of the regions, provinces, and republics, to the Supreme Council of the USSR—a two-house parliament that meets four months a year. Election for each of the soviets is by universal, direct, secret ballot of those who have reached the age of eighteen.

When the Supreme Council is not in session, its broad powers are administered by a Presidium of thirty-seven members. Appointed by, and responsible to the Supreme Council, are also the members of the Council of Peoples' Commissars, in charge of the executive departments (mainly economic) of the government. The judicial system is composed of judges chosen by direct election to preside over a hierarchy of courts ranging from the local Peoples' Courts to the Supreme Court of the USSR.

THE COMMUNIST PARTY

The formality of Soviet government is meaningless without an appreciation of the dominant role of the Communist Party, "engineers of the revolution and architects of the new society." Officially, the Party is separate from the government; it has no legal mandate to rule. But in practice, members of the Party fill the large majority of responsible government posts throughout the Soviet Union. Policy on every important issue is first formulated in meetings of Party members; the resultant decisions, or "directives," are then rendered into law or executive orders by Party members acting in their governmental capacities.

The enormous power and prestige of the Communist Party derive from the fact that it successfully carried through the revolution, that it constantly draws into its ranks the most promising younger leaders, that it is a compact, highly disciplined unit, and operates with striking singleness of purpose. Units of the Party are distributed in virtually every industrial, political, and military center of the nation. No important decision may be taken, no venture embarked upon, no conflict arbitrated, without reference to the local Party "cell"

or its officials.   In any question of proper Marxian inter-
pretation, the Communist Party is the final authority.

Membership in the Party is at present somewhat over
two millions.   New recruits are drawn mainly from the
ranks of youth organizations, the Comsomols (aged
fifteen to thirty) and the Young Pioneers (ten to
fifteen).

POSITION OF STALIN

Officially, Stalin holds only nominal rank as an elected
delegate to the Supreme Council.   His immense power
in guiding the destinies of the Soviet State is derived
from his position as General Secretary of the Communist Party, its most important post and one he has held
since 1922.   Since official state policy is actually formulated by Party leaders, and among these Stalin holds a
pre-eminent position, the reality of his influence is evident.   As one of the inheritors of Lenin's power, Stalin
attained supremacy over his chief rival, Leon Trotsky,
on the issue of "building Socialism at home," rather
than pressing for immediate world revolution.[2]   In the
last analysis, Stalin's power is granted by, and subject
to, the decisions of the Communist Party of the Soviet
Union, which is itself the unchallenged policy-making
force in the nation.

---

[2] Until his recent death in exile in Mexico, Trotsky conducted a
world-wide campaign of opposition to the present Soviet regime and
its program, accusing its leaders of having "betrayed the revolution"
and of having departed from the principles of Marxism. The organization of this opposition bears the name "Fourth International," to
distinguish it from the Third (Communist) International.

GOVERNMENT AND INDUSTRY

The Soviet Union is a society in which all important political, economic, and social institutions are consciously co-ordinated to serve broad public objectives. The government must be understood as combining both political and economic control. The ownership of the land, resources, and means of production resides in the state as a whole; industrial processes are carried on under the direction of commissariats, or departments, according to a unified plan for the entire economy. Ultimate control of industry is thus highly centralized, with some initiative left to the management, trade unions, and local Party unit in each enterprise. Besides state-owned industry, which predominates, there exists a sizable number of producers' co-operatives, and a scattering of self-employed craftsmen and peasants.

Agriculture, still the largest single industry in the Soviet Union, has been almost entirely collectivized. Two major forms of organization prevail: First are the state farms, thousands of acres in size, owned and operated by the government, with workers receiving stipulated wages. By far the more important section consists of co-operative farm associations, to whom permanent possession of the land is granted by the state. In addition to sharing in the collective income, each family retains a small plot of land for private use.

Distribution outlets for consumers' goods consist of state-owned stores and co-operative units—the first stationed chiefly in the cities, the second in villages. Com-

modity prices for both are fixed within a narrow range
for each community or geographical section.

FINANCIAL SYSTEM

Banks, credit, and currency are all to be found in the
Soviet Union, but their function differs from that of
private enterprise. Banking facilities are nationalized.
The currency system is "managed" or controlled by the
state for domestic purposes only, without reference to
foreign valuations. At the center of the banking system
is the state bank, with its thousands of local branches
and subsidiaries. These serve as perpetual clearing-
houses for the exchange of debits and credits between
enterprises, for the financing of new construction,
municipal ventures, and foreign trade—as well as for
banks of deposit.

ECONOMIC PLANNING

Ownership of the means of production implies their
use by the state according to a definite, co-ordinated
plan. An All-Union Planning Commission accumu-
lates data on every conceivable phase of the economy,
balancing consumers' demands with the resources available for production. A detailed "five-year plan" is peri-
odically drawn up (the third of these, 1938–42, is now
in progress) and blueprints furnished to each enterprise
concerned with its fulfilment.

The first five-year plan was devoted to constructing a
base for socialized industry in the fields of power development, capital goods, and technical training of
workers. The second and third plans continued this

trend but shifted the emphasis to an increased production of consumers' goods and services.

UNIONS, WAGES, AND SECURITY

Soviet labor organization follows the industrial form, with all classes of workers in a plant included within a single union and all such units federated into councils that parallel the political structure. About 80 per cent of industrial workers are thus enrolled.

Unions are jointly responsible with management (and with local Communist Party units) for satisfactory production and shop discipline. In addition, the unions negotiate collective working agreements, administer pension and insurance funds, and conduct a variety of educational and recreational activities. Strikes are not forbidden but seldom occur, owing to enforced arbitration.

General wage scales are formulated for each industry by the controlling commissariat, then converted into specific pay schedules by agreement between the union and the plant management. Rates of pay follow the socialist principle of reward on the basis of individual worth. General wage levels are directly linked to the productive output of the whole economy, and are determined by the funds remaining from total state income after capital investment and other expenses have been subtracted. Noneconomic rewards in the form of public recognition and distinctions are stressed.

A comprehensive social-security program, with costs borne by the state, is administered by trade unions for their members. Benefits include retirement pensions, child and maternal welfare, disability compensation, etc. Health care and hospitalization are free services.

EDUCATION AND PROPAGANDA

In Marxian theory, the stage of socialism is a training period during which collectivist principles and institutions gradually supplant those of capitalist society. The school system is but one medium through which this transvaluation is to be effected—the press, theater, workshop, collective farm, political forum, are all co-ordinated toward the same end. Industrial enterprises often act as "sponsors" of community schools; special emphasis is placed on "learning by doing." The dominant theme is that of collective responsibility, as opposed to the urge for personal advancement.

Education in a broad sense thus consists of inculcating socialist values in young and old and, in this respect, is indistinguishable from propaganda. The Soviet press and radio serve a similar purpose in mobilizing public opinion toward achieving official socialist objectives. The practice of "socialist self-criticism," widely indulged in by the press and other agencies, is an attempt to compensate for the outlawry of opposition points of view. Freedom of discussion on any issue of public policy is permitted only until an official decision is announced; then it must cease. But at no time is the basic character of socialist society allowed to be challenged.

SOME GENERAL PRINCIPLES AND ATTITUDES

Even the briefest description of Soviet institutions requires more space than is available here, but the following additional features deserve mention.

State ownership of property extends only to that which is used to produce and distribute goods; property for direct use by consumers, such as food, clothing, a house, books, is privately owned by individuals or by co-operative associations.

A fundamental tenet of Marxian socialism is that of complete equality of all persons, regardless of race, nationality, or sex, insofar as their social, political, legal, and economic status is concerned.

The Soviet view of crime and punishment stresses the importance of social environment upon human behavior. Individuals found guilty of crimes against *persons* are sent, for relatively short periods, to rehabilitation camps, where they engage in constructing public works. But crimes against the *state,* such as counter-revolutionary acts, exploitation of others, and theft of collective property, are subject to extreme penalties.

The church as an institution has been deprived of its educational and social functions. Religious worship is permitted, but the state encourages private antireligious organizations and their activities. Religion itself is regarded as an "opiate," tending to divert man's attention from his earthly responsibilities by the promise of spiritual rewards. Communism claims the ability to realize human brotherhood through a form of social organization that will promote a maximum expression of human ideals.

Similarly, communists declare that genuine democracy is unattainable within capitalistic institutions; that political equality is only an illusion so long as economic inequality prevails; and that only with the triumph of public ownership and the dissolving of class divisions can freedom for all men be assured. Thus, communism claims to be not the denial but the fufilment of democracy in its completest sense.

FOREIGN POLICY AND THE COMINTERN

Soviet foreign policy is dictated by a single aim, to extend communism throughout the rest of the world. The first consideration, however, is to establish a successful example of socialism at home and to safeguard the nation against the real or fancied threats of the capitalistic world. The second is to encourage the efforts of revolutionary working-class movements in other countries and thereby to make new acquisitions to socialist society.

The communist parties which have been formed in a number of countries are guided in their revolutionary strategy by the Third International (Comintern), to which all are affiliated. Activities toward the attainment of socialism depend upon conditions prevailing in each country but include, wherever possible, working through labor unions, political parties, reform organizations, and propaganda agencies. Pending the arrival of a revolutionary situation, communist parties attempt to strengthen the position of the working class and to mold it into a conscious instrument of social change.

The Comintern is not a branch of the Soviet government, but has its residence in Moscow and takes its direction primarily from the Communist Party of the Soviet Union.

CHAPTER VIII

Anarchism

ANARCHISM is the doctrine which proposes that society shall be reorganized on the basis of small, self-governing communities in which the land, capital, and machinery of production will be owned in common, and the power of the political state abolished in order that the fullest measure of individual liberty and equality may prevail.

The anarchist movement is directed against these two institutions of modern society: first, the private ownership of those instruments and resources that produce essential goods and services; second, the concentration of political authority in governmental agencies. The first of these is blamed for the existence of widespread economic injustice, insecurity, imperialism, and the breakdown of social morality. But the political state, anarchists believe, is no less destructive of society, since in all its forms, parliamentary as well as autocratic, it serves as the agent through which the exploitation of the people is effected and sanctioned.

SUPREME INDIVIDUALISM

The doctrine of anarchism represents the most extreme form of individualism. It conceives of man as naturally good and just, rational in his outlook, cooperative in his relationships with others. The natural

75

impulse of such individuals, when free to follow their own promptings, is to combine voluntarily in functional groups for their mutual welfare. So long as these associations remain voluntary, uncorrupted by force and coercion, the essential goodness of the individual will prevail. In the absence of compulsion, each will deal fairly with the others, and in the resultant social harmony the freest development of each will be secured.

But the conditions for such a society, anarchists contend, have been nullified by the growth of the political state and the institution of private property.[1] The consequence is that in all societies men have become enslaved to those who rule and exploited by those who own.

ROLE OF THE STATE

To the anarchist, institutionalism and authority are parasites feeding on human freedom. The inherent satisfaction of men in their work has become debased by the wage system. Personal and social behavior are enclosed in a network of legal restrictions, and even morality is administered by an organized church. Modern society is built on a basis of force. Only a shred of personal freedom remains, with the result that human beings become systematically demoralized. Anarchists regard the criminal in society as one who is not inherently bad but is rather the victim of social maladjustment. In such cases, punishment is not a remedy; it is society that needs change.

---

[1] "Private property," as used here, refers solely to the ownership of capital and the means of production, not to property for personal use. See section entitled "Private Property" in Chap. III.

The leading role in this drama of oppression is acted by the political state. But the state itself, anarchists maintain, was created from the first by the owners of property to protect and legalize their exploitation of the masses. The law that it enforces is the attempt to make permanent the existing property relationships. Representative government is admitted to be less brutal in this respect than autocracy, but its purposes are the same. So long as one group holds the power to dominate others through political or economic control, the rest of mankind is enslaved.

The anarchist conclusion is that, in order to re-establish the conditions of human freedom, the twin evils of private property and the political state must be abolished.

ANARCHIST SOCIETY

In their stead would be established a society composed of small-sized, voluntary associations of individuals engaging in all the necessary activities of life—the production and distribution of goods, education, recreation, the fine arts, military defense, and so on. Some of the groups would be local only; others would be federated into regional, national, or international associations as desired, but would still retain local autonomy. Communities would resemble to some extent the workmen's guilds and free cities of the Middle Ages, and the federations, for their part, would simply broaden the fields in which many voluntary associations now operate nationally and internationally. There would be no place for the church as an organized institution, since anarchists hold that social morality is inherent in the individual and requires no organized form.

In each community the land, machinery, utilities, natural resources, and equipment used for the production of goods would be owned in common, or jointly if desired, by agreement with other communities. The wage system—that is, the employment of workers by owners at specified wages—would give way to co-operative production and equalized income. Private ownership of goods or property, such as food, a house, an automobile, or anything not used to produce other goods, would be freely permitted. The principle of mutual aid, natural to all men, would replace the rule of force. Whatever conflicts of a personal or social nature arose in a community would be settled peaceably by local boards of arbitration.

ABSENCE OF GOVERNMENT

The absence of government does not, according to the anarchist, mean the absence of order. On the contrary, the state of disorder existing in society everywhere is claimed to be the consequence of the "legal force" imposed upon the population by the state. When this rule of force is abolished, the natural co-operativeness of men will take the place of organized repression. Government over men will give way to the impersonal administration of things.

PHILOSOPHICAL ANARCHISM

Although the majority of anarchists are agreed on this general form of the new society, there is a major division of thought on the important issue of the means to be used in effecting a transition from the present capitalistic state to the self-governing community. The Philosophical (sometimes called Individualist or Christian) Anarchists preach a moral and spiritual transformation of the individual as the way to social change. Since coercive government and private-property ownership result in social disruption, this school of thought advocates a voluntary renunciation of both institutions, in the belief that the transition will thus be made peaceably. Passive disobedience and a return to the spirit of the teachings of Jesus are variously proposed. Philosophical anarchism is unalterably opposed to the use of force or of revolutionary means to attain its ends. Coercion is condemned, no matter for what purpose. Individuals must transform themselves first, then influence others by precept and example.

Because in its very nature philosophical anarchism rejects organized action, it has exerted no important force as a social movement. Certain of its teachings, however, have been widely accepted as a standard of ideal social conduct.

COMMUNIST ANARCHISM

Communist anarchism, by far the more important division of the movement, combines the philosophy of anarchism with the revolutionary program of communism. The most important factor in this doctrine is a recognition of the class struggle[2] between the property

---

[2] See "Class Struggle" in Chap. V.

owners and workers in society. No final victory in this struggle is held to be possible until the owners and their political agents are dispossessed.

But the transition, according to this view, cannot occur within the individual himself; nor will the state, which seeks always to perpetuate itself, consent to its own destruction. No choice remains but to employ revolutionary methods. Political action is rejected as useless, either for immediate or long-range reform. Instead, the workers organized in powerful trade unions are to be drilled in the tactics of "direct action," to use whatever means will be found effective in weakening, and eventually bringing to an end, the existing state. The strike, boycott, and sabotage are some of the methods to be used, but the workers must not be allowed to forget that each of these actions is merely a preliminary for the eventual seizure of property and the dispossession of the ruling class. (It should be noted, however, that the portrait of the typical anarchist as a hate-possessed, bomb-throwing individual is greatly distorted. The practice of deliberate terrorism attributed to anarchists was a short-lived interlude of the late nineteenth century, inspired by the extremist leaders M. Bakunin and J. Most. Attempts at assassination of prominent officials were declared to be justified as a protest against the "office" of the victim, not the individual himself. In that office, anarchists professed to see the symbol of political and economic injustice. But the large majority of anarchists have refused to subscribe to this justification of violence.)

COMMUNISM DISTINGUISHED FROM COMMUNIST ANARCHISM

Two important distinctions may be seen between communism and communist anarchism. It was these distinctions that caused the historic schism between the followers of Marx and of Bakunin. The first difference is found in the fact that communism stresses the need of political, as well as economic, action against the existing state. The second is, that, although both doctrines agree that their ideal aim is a stateless, classless society, communists contend that for a period after capitalism is destroyed it will be necessary to maintain a new state, controlled in this case by and for the working class, to direct the problems of reconstruction and suppress counterrevolution. But anarchists insist upon the avoidance of any state whatsoever and call for the immediate decentralization of society into small, voluntary, independent units. Only under such conditions, they believe, can the individual ever realize the freedom and equality to which he is by nature entitled.

Anarchism seeks to reconcile economic collectivism with personal freedom by removing what it believes to be the two barriers to that goal—profit-motivated enterprise and political power. Communism claims to do the same, but only after passing through a transitional period of proletarian dictatorship.

HISTORICAL DECLINE

Anarchism today is a negligible movement. Its doctrine and program began to achieve prominence just before the middle of the nineteenth century, but by the close of the First World War little of its influence remained. Anarchist groups are still to be found in the Latin countries of Europe—Italy, Spain, and France—where the movement attained its greatest strength.

CHAPTER IX

Syndicalism

S YNDICALISM is a combined doctrine and program of
revolutionary change centering about the unique
function of industrial labor unions in abolishing
the wage system of capitalism and inaugurating a democratic producers' commonwealth.

ORIGINS

It is evident that syndicalism resembles closely two
other social doctrines, anarchism and socialism, from
which, in fact, syndicalism was largely derived. The
syndicalist movement arose in France during the last
decade of the nineteenth century as a reflection of the
dissatisfaction of organized labor with the repeated be-
trayals of its program by political reformists. Leaders
of the new movement enlisted the support of Marxian
socialists in devising an independent program.

The resulting doctrine, which has been stated most
clearly by George Sorel, became a fusion of Marxism
and anarchism. From the former, syndicalists accepted
the idea of the economic basis of society, the analysis of
surplus value, and the thesis of the class struggle; from
the latter, the emphasis on individualism and rejection
of the political state. As an improvement upon both,
syndicalist doctrine added some refinements: the principle of the creative character of labor, functional repre-

sentation, the predominant role of industrial unions, and the tactic of the general strike.

MAN AS PRODUCER

Syndicalism conceives of society as fundamentally an association of wealth producers. Each individual is a necessary part of the economic scheme, and it is his function as a producer that determines his social attitude. However, to the syndicalist, productiveness means infinitely more than just the expenditure of mind and muscle for material reward. He preaches a "gospel of work," a pride in creation for its own sake. Labor is held to be an inherently moral act, the truest expression of personality. Its reward comes from a sense of accomplishment, not from the expectation of monetary gain.

But the consequence of the capitalist wage system, according to syndicalists, is that the natural impulses of men to labor creatively are actually suppressed. Production has become a purely commercial and mechanical transaction. The necessity to work in order that others may profit destroys personal incentive. Pride in personal accomplishment is sacrificed to the passion for gain. Labor sinks to the status of a necessary evil, and its opposite, the prospect of leisure, becomes the controlling aim of wealth production.

The great mass of workers, who are the real producers, are granted no voice in the management of industry. Their skills are purchased at a price, like any commodity. Their value is measured not as human beings but as costs of production. These are the consequences that arise from the processes of capitalism, in which the

ownership of the machinery of production enables the
ruling class to cheat the workers of their creativeness
and of their rightful rewards.

Syndicalism is thus completely Marxian in posing the
historical struggle between the owning and working
classes. In fact, no other doctrine pursues this issue of
the class struggle so relentlessly. Its existence is held to
be the fundamental reality, and the destruction of capitalism is believed possible only when the workers, recognizing the inherent conflict between labor and capital,
unite to expropriate their oppressors.

METHODS OF ACTION

Syndicalism, in line with its labor origin and emphasis, advocates exclusively economic action in its program of change. Like anarchism, it rejects political
tactics of every sort. It professes no more faith in
parliamentary government than in autocracy, contending that the state is invariably an agency for upholding
the capitalist class in its exploitation.

The workers must therefore rely upon themselves to
attain the objective of syndicalism. They are to be organized not into a political party but into labor unions
on the industrial plan—that is, unions which include in
one grouping all the workers, skilled and unskilled, in
each industry. Through these agencies, militant warfare is to be waged against the two common enemies,
employers and state. The weapons of the workers will
be their industrial power: the boycott, union label,
sabotage, and, most important of all, the strike. Each
of these weapons will be used only incidentally to gain

improved working conditions; primarily they will be designed to increase working-class solidarity, to test the strength of unions, and to weaken the position of employers. Each preliminary strike is to be regarded merely as a rehearsal for the supreme effort of the workers, the general strike. This will be used when the unions have become powerful enough to cause a complete stoppage of vital industrial functions. At such a time, syndicalists believe, it will be possible for the workers to dispossess the capitalists and to seize control of the national economy. At the same time, as a consequence of antimilitarist activity, the state will be deprived of its armed forces and compelled to surrender control. The way then will be cleared for the inauguration of a new social system.

THE SYNDICALIST COMMONWEALTH

Syndicalist society, like that of anarchism, is intended to provide a maximum of opportunity for the free development of the individual and the exercise of his creative abilities. Like anarchism also, the social structure would consist of a loose federation of self-governing communities.

But under syndicalism the emphasis in this respect is again placed primarily on the function of the industrial unions, which will be the focal points of economic, social, and cultural life. The organized workers in each division of industry, including agriculture, would own their land, factories, and production machinery in common. There would be no segregation of employers from employees, no wage system or profit-making, no living on unearned income. The rewards of production would be shared co-operatively.

Every instrument of coercive government—as bitterly opposed by syndicalists as by anarchists—would be abolished. The necessary duties of administration would be assumed by labor union councils. In all such agencies representation would be on a functional basis—that is, on the basis of occupational membership rather than of mere geographical residence. Communities would be independent, self-governing; they might become federated for any necessary purposes, but centralized authority would be strictly avoided.

SPREAD OF SYNDICALISM

Syndicalist doctrine found its most sympathetic acceptance in the Latin nations of Europe, France, Italy, and Spain. In the first of these its program was for a time energetically furthered by the French General Confederation of Labor. In present-day Italy, the structure of the Fascist corporative state shows the syndicalist influence, especially in the principle of functional representation.[1] In Spain, both anarchist and syndicalist groups survived the First World War to participate actively in the overthrow of the Bourbon monarchy in 1931 and in the subsequent reconstruction period. A modification of syndicalist doctrine, guild socialism,[2] gained

---

[1] This reference should not be taken as implying an actual relationship between fascism and syndicalism. The fascist corporative structure is a creature of the political state; in it the syndicalist principles of self-government, common ownership, and social equality are conspicuously lacking.

[2] See Chap. X.

wide prominence in Great Britain in the early part of
the present century but became a casualty of the war
years.

THE I.W.W.

In the United States, syndicalism took shape with the
organizing of the Industrial Workers of the World
(I.W.W.) in 1905. Its strength was recruited largely
from among the agricultural workers, lumber camps,
and longshoremen. Its formation was in part a protest
against the exclusiveness of the American Federation of
Labor, which concentrated on craft unionism and
ignored the masses of semiskilled and unskilled workers
throughout the country.

I.W.W. leaders stressed the industrial form of unionism and adopted a thoroughgoing syndicalist program,
both in its tactics and its aims. Membership in the
organization probably never exceeded 60,000, but it
represented a militant labor leadership capable of enlist-
ing large numbers of sympathetic workers on critical
issues. The I.W.W. movement declined rapidly in the
immediate postwar years, owing to the active opposition
of the United States government.

SYNDICALISM AND COMMUNISM

Although syndicalism is at several points identified
with communism, certain distinctions should be noted.
First, it restricts its revolutionary tactics entirely to the
economic field, despising political action. Second, it
repudiates completely the authority of the state, whether
it be the agency of the capitalists or of the workers.

Finally, it puts its full faith in industrial labor organizations, both for the struggle against capitalism and in the creation of the new society.

In many respects, as mentioned above, syndicalism is close to anarchism; it has, in fact, been aptly described as "organized anarchy."

CHAPTER X

Guild Socialism

GUILD SOCIALISM is a plan for the reorganization of society on a functional economic basis, with the principal means of production owned in common and with each unit of industry operated under a system of self-government by the workers.

ATTITUDE TOWARD CAPITALISM AND STATE

The term "guild" is derived from the associations of merchants and tradesmen that flourished throughout the cities of Europe during the Middle Ages and were influential in securing for their membership a considerable degree of economic and political freedom.

The advocates of guild socialism have undertaken to harmonize the demands of personal liberty with the requirements of economic collectivism. They concur with the socialist indictment of capitalism as a system that breeds social injustice and agree that the instruments of production must be transferred to the common ownership of the people. The aims of a democratic commonwealth, they maintain, cannot be realized until the workers are released from their bondage to the wage system.

But in agreement with syndicalist doctrine, to which guild socialism is indebted for its main elements, the political state is distrusted just as deeply as is the insti-

tution of private property. Political authority is held
to be everywhere uncongenial to human freedom.
Nothing, it is believed, would be gained by substituting
a socialist bureaucracy for that of capitalist control.
Authority must somehow be decentralized to the point
where the acceptance of group decisions will be as nearly
unanimous as possible. The smaller the social grouping,
the more readily this can be done. Society, according to
the guild socialists, is a pluralistic affair: it consists not
of a single, uniform association but of a large number
of diverse groupings of persons reflecting their various
interests—as producers, as consumers, as citizens, and
the like. Each of these groupings should be free to
make its own rules and conduct its own affairs insofar
as possible. Political authority over the whole people
should be limited strictly to such matters of general
concern as the handling of foreign affairs and the requirements of national defense.

GUILD SOCIALIST SOCIETY

The guild socialist program may be seen as embracing
two major objectives. First, the ownership of the principal means of production must be transferred to the
trusteeship of the people as a whole. Following this,
the social structure is to be reorganized on a basis of
functional self-government, wherein the political authority will be severely curtailed.[1]

The economy of the proposed society in the several

---

[1] The proposal has sometimes been made that political authority be
removed altogether, as in syndicalism, but this view has gained little
support among guild socialists.

fields of production, distribution, and finance would be centered about the operations of a number of "guilds," or self-governing associations of workers. Each group in a factory or other unit would be free to organize locally, elect its managers, and conduct its own affairs. Local guilds would be represented by delegates in a regional guild for that industry; and each region, in turn, would be represented in a national guild congress to which would be entrusted the planning, co-ordination, and supervision of the whole economy.

The method of selecting delegates for guild purposes is that of occupational (or "functional"), rather than mere geographical, representation. Guild socialists claim the superiority of this practice over that generally prevailing, contending that no single representative can adequately speak for the wide diversity of interests—political, economic, social—to be found among his constituents.

The guild structure, representing persons in their capacity of producers, is expected to constitute but one of two co-equal governing bodies for the nation. The second, elected by geographical constituencies, is designed to perform the same service for the whole population as citizens and consumers. The result would be a two-chambered congress or parliament, each chamber empowered to act in its defined sphere. Conflicts of jurisdiction would be settled by a joint committee.

GUILD ACTIVITIES

Whereas the ownership of industry under guild socialism would reside in the whole people, its actual operation would be entrusted to the local guilds of workers, managers, and technicians. Every effort would be made to encourage the creative abilities of guild members, whose incentive to work, it is alleged, has suffered under the existing wage system. Employer-employee relationships would no longer exist. Guild members would possess equal voting rights, with important matters of procedure subject to popular decision. Each guild would pay an annual rental, or tax, to the state for the use of its property or franchise. Net earnings of the guild enterprises would be distributed to members on a profit-sharing basis. Price control over production would be exercised by the national guild congress.

METHODS OF TRANSITION

Guild socialists are more optimistic than the syndicalists in expecting a transition to the new society by gradual, evolutionary means. The agency of change is the same, that of the trade unions, transformed into comprehensive industrial units conscious of their power and objectives. Political action is altogether avoided.

The industrial-union structure is to be projected as widely as possible; using this weapon, the workers will promote a policy of "encroaching control" in each industry and seek the gradual transfer of powers from the owners to the unions. At the same time, pressure will be exerted upon the state to acquire increasing ownership of production plants, with allowance for fair compensation. Forced transfer would be resorted to only if necessary to overcome resistance. The whole program is intended to achieve its aims without encountering the issue of violence.

ORIGINS

Guild socialism is an almost exclusively British version of syndicalism, brought into being just prior to the outbreak of the First World War. From the first, its leaders set themselves the task of planning a social framework in which the existing conflicts of producer *vs.* consumer and state *vs.* individual might be resolved. The harshness of syndicalist tactics was tempered by the doctrine of gradualness; the state was not to be eliminated altogether, but to be counterbalanced by industrial self-government. In common with orthodox socialism, the ownership of production property was to be vested in the people, but the evils of bureaucracy were to be forestalled by decentralized control.

Guild socialist doctrine became for a time the official program of the British labor movement, and a series of guild ventures were established. But the postwar depression, which resulted in the weakening of the British trade unions and the intensification of political control, brought about a swift decline. Nevertheless, the influence of guild socialist thought has been extensive, and some aspects of its organizational principles have already been applied to industry.

CHAPTER XI

Fabianism
(Fabian Socialism)

FABIANISM[1] deserves a place among reform movements as representing the typically moderate, rational, middle-class point of view. The name Fabianism is given to the doctrine that has since 1884 occupied the efforts of the Fabian Society of Great Britain, a small but influential group of socialists claiming such leaders as Sidney and Beatrice Webb, George Bernard Shaw, H. G. Wells, and G. D. H. Cole. The Society continues today almost exclusively as a social research institution, but its policies have been translated into the program of the British Labour Party.

The goal of Fabianism is that of a socialist society, but this is virtually its only connection with Marxism. The path it proposes to follow is purely one of reform, and that by way of political methods alone. In this respect, Fabianism stands as far to the "right" of socialism as the latter does in regard to communism.

ECONOMIC THEORY

In economic theory, the Fabians adhere rather to the

---

[1] The name is derived from Quintus Fabius Maximus, surnamed Cunctator (delayer), the Roman general famous for his successful tactics of delaying the enemy and refusing to give direct battle during the defense of Rome against Hannibal.

tradition of the nineteenth-century Utilitarians than
to the more vigorous departures of Karl Marx.
Whereas Marxians claim that the value of all economic
goods is determined by the amount of labor necessary
to produce them, Fabians find that the value of goods
depends rather upon their social utility. This necessarily invalidates the Marxian theory of surplus value
as an explanation of how the owners of capital exploit
their workers. Fabians trace the injustices of capitalism
instead to the privilege acquired by owners of property
to profit exclusively from the values created by all.

Particular stress is placed on the differential rents
obtained from land ownership. It is claimed that the
actual value of land, whether for crops, residences, or
industrial purposes, is created by the whole community
through its very existence; consequently, private land-
lords should not alone be permitted to reap the benefits.[2]
Similarly, it is held that the efforts of both labor power
and capital are so fundamentally social in all their consequences that their use for private gain is wholly un-
justified. Fabians therefore maintain that the land and
the machinery of production ought to be owned in
common, so that society as a whole could benefit from
their use.

METHODS OF CHANGE

Fabian reform tactics are inspired by a faith in
progress and the continuity of social development. Its

[2] This theory of land values is traceable to the influence of the Eng-
lish economist, David Ricardo, and the American, Henry George, the
latter remembered for his "single tax" proposal.

leaders are convinced that men are enough rational and
sensible of their common welfare to accept whatever
improvements can be demonstrated as necessary. They
point to the considerable body of legislation enacted in
response to social need—acts for housing, insurance,
medical care, conditions of work, minimum wages—in
proof of this thesis. Fabians are confident that as the
desirability of socializing the land and industries of the
nation is made apparent, public opinion will be per-
suaded to embark on the program. The process would
be one of gradual "permeation" of those groups directly
concerned with economic policy: trade unions, political
parties, government officials, technicians, managers, even
employers. In a sense, all pressure would be political,
since Fabians look to the parliamentary state to vote
in socialism by stages—being confident that the extension of suffrage and representative government have
made such action possible.

In general, independent industrial action by trade
unions is not encouraged. Every effort toward change
must be translated into political form and exerted upon
those engaged in governing and administering the state.
Fabians emphatically reject the tactics of class warfare;
they do not foresee the inevitable breakdown of capitalism; and they are only remotely conscious of the special
mission of the working class in effecting change. Fabian
socialism is to issue from the enlightened co-operation
of social classes, whereas Marxian socialism is intended
to result from the conflict of opposed classes. In its
entire spirit, as well as its methodology, Fabianism remains at the opposite pole from Marxism.

CHAPTER XII

Christian Socialism

C HRISTIAN SOCIALISM is the doctrine held by those
who reject the elements of capitalist society and
accept the program of socialism as consistent with
Christian principles.

ORIGINS

Some form of this belief has existed since before the
advent of socialism itself, but the first attempt to com-
mit the church to a program of social change was intro-
duced in England in 1848 with the formation of the
Christian Socialist Movement. Its founders, notably
Frederick Maurice, Charles Kingsley, and Vansittart
Neale, were impressed with the widespread destitution
among the British working class and traced this condition to the evils arising from ownership of private
property and the struggle for profits. Convinced that
capitalism as a system violated the fundamentals of
Christianity, the Christian Socialists sought to enlist the
energies of the church in a program of reform. Their
aim was to communalize private property and, this
achieved, to set up self-governing industrial groups
that would own their equipment and share their income
equally. The Christian Socialist Movement failed of
its object, and the same fate overtook later experiments
of a similar nature.

At the present time Christian socialism exists, not as an organized "movement," but as a set of convictions professed by leaders and adherents of numerous religious groups. Lacking an organizational form of their own, except in local cases, Christian Socialists operate as individuals or as members of other groups devoted to similar ends.

CHRISTIAN SOCIALIST DOCTRINE

Consequently, Christian socialism represents neither an integrated doctrine nor a systematic program. What is common to all its adherents is the conviction that the teachings of Christ provide a basis for social, as well as personal, relationships; that these teachings further imply a type of society which approximates that of socialism and is at complete variance with predatory capitalism; and that the duty rests upon sincere Christians to bring about the desired change. The purposes of God and man can be served only, it is maintained, when community interests are given priority over those of the individual; when the uses of property are defined by the common good; when acquisitiveness has given way to the satisfaction of human need; and when the principles of co-operation take the place of competitive struggle. When these aims are realized, it is believed that human brotherhood, which is at the core of the Christian faith, will have become possible. The socialist commonwealth is therefore desired not for itself nor even as a necessarily permanent condition but for its contribution to the ethical and religious life of man.

CHRISTIAN SOCIALIST SOCIETY

A maximum of diversity exists as to the form of society contemplated. Proposals range from that of a "reformed" capitalism to that of a purely communistic type, in which all kinds of property would be held in common. The majority clearly favors a kind of socialism in which the agencies of production, distribution, and exchange would be owned in common and guided by a central planning board, but with actual operations carried on by self-governing producers' associations.[1] Emphasis would be placed on the dignity of human labor and the social values of co-operative enterprise.

METHODS OF TRANSITION

While recognizing the present conflict of economic classes under capitalism, Christian Socialists reject Marx's advocacy of revolutionary change.[2] Efforts are devoted to the general improvement of working-class conditions, educational activities, encouragement of labor unions, action through political parties, and particularly the formation of co-operative enterprises. By these methods it is hoped to eradicate the worst evils of capitalistic society and eventually to combine the moral force of the church with the political power of the state to accomplish a transition to socialism.

---

[1] See the sections entitled "Building the Socialist Economy" and "Economic Agencies" in Chap. VI.

[2] There are some exceptions to this attitude, as there are also exceptions to the generally accepted pacifist position of Christian Socialists; forcible change, as a last resort, is considered by some to be justified if necessary to uphold legal processes.

The essence of Christian socialism is to be found in its religious impulsion. Its participation in social change stems from the conviction that the teachings of Christ require a remolding of human institutions in order to be fully realized. From this fact is derived the denial of capitalist society and acceptance of socialism as a substitute—as well as the means to be used toward that end. From this same point of reference, Christian socialism denies the theory of historical materialism[3] as the sole explanation of social change. But with equal vigor it affirms that Christianity implies social responsibility and that material factors have a vital bearing on the ability to live a religious life. Personal faith in a God must not become an escape from the realities of human existence. The Christian imperative must operate equally in all areas, personal and social, or it will become wholly sterile.

The Christian Socialist doctrines have spread, in varying forms, to the membership of Protestant, Catholic, and Jewish groups throughout the world. It may be considered an important influence in the United States, Canada, and Great Britain. On the European continent, however, Christian Socialist trade unions and political parties have sometimes been formed for the express purpose of counteracting the successes of Marxian socialism.

---

[3] See Chap. V.

CHAPTER XIII

Italian Fascism[1]

T HE KEY to an understanding of fascism lies in its conception of the state as a dominant, all-inclusive organism, which gives direction to every form of national existence. As opposed to liberal-democratic theory, wherein the state owes its creation to popular sovereignty, fascism conceives a state that is itself the source of all power and to which the people are wholly subordinate.

The fascist state is described as an absolute, to which all things are relative. Mussolini speaks of it as both a material and a spiritual force, superior to any person, group, or even generation, and holding in its custody the glories of the past and the promise of the future.[2] The fascist state is the supreme truth, the basis of morality, and the criterion of social values. It claims a monopoly of national effort, demanding the undivided loyalty of its subjects. "Everything within the state, nothing outside the state, nothing against the state." In this fact

---

[1] The term "fascism" is derived from *fascio*, meaning a group or bundle. In the shape of a bundle of sticks tied together, the symbol is indicative of strength in unity, as contrasted with the weakness of each separate stick.

[2] The reader who finds this abstraction difficult to grasp will obtain some comfort from the following statement by Mussolini about the state:

"We have created our myth. . . . It is not necessary that it shall be a reality. It is a reality by the fact that it is a goad, that it is a hope, that it is faith, that it is courage."

lies its totalitarian nature: it comprehends every aspect of human life and controls them all for its avowed purposes.

THE FASCIST PARTY

In theory, the fascist state is a mystical sort of higher law in process of unfoldment. Necessarily, the abstraction must be given life; the practical tasks of government require concrete forms. The power to do this rests with the Fascist Party, a small, selective elite, or ruling class, of which Mussolini is the head. The Fascist Party is not only the single legal political agency but, unlike the Communist Party of the Soviet Union, is the official arm of the Italian government. For practical purposes, the state and the Party are identical.

The Party is a close-knit, highly disciplined unit, organized on military lines, pledged to unquestioning obedience to its leader. To it is entrusted the function of organizing the governmental structure and co-ordinating every activity, social, political, and economic, within its scope.

STRUCTURE OF GOVERNMENT

The structure of government may be likened to a pyramid, with power descending from the top.[3] At the apex stands Mussolini, *Il Duce del Governo,* "Head of the Government" and of the Fascist Party. A cabinet of fourteen ministers, supervising the various functions of

---

[3] Technically, the liberally conceived Constitution of 1848 is still in effect, but its provisions have been largely suspended. The Italian King-Emperor, Victor Emmanuel III, remains the acknowledged head of the state, but the powers of governing rest entirely with Mussolini.

THE GOVERNMENT OF FASCIST ITALY

The Government of Fascist Italy

THE KING — TITULAR HEAD

CONSTITUTION OF 1848

THE STATE

THE CORPORATE STATE

MINISTER OF CORPORATIONS MUSSOLINI

NATIONAL COUNCIL OF CORPORATIONS

22 CORPORATIONS

EMPLOYERS' ASSOCIATIONS

NATIONAL CONFEDERATION OF EMPLOYERS

PROVINCIAL FEDERATIONS OF EMPLOYERS

LOCAL SYNDICATES OF EMPLOYERS

EMPLOYEES' ASSOCIATIONS

NATIONAL CONFEDERATION OF EMPLOYEES

PROVINCIAL FEDERATIONS OF EMPLOYEES

LOCAL SYNDICATES OF EMPLOYEES

THE FASCIST PARTY

PARTY LEADER MUSSOLINI

FASCIST GRAND COUNCIL

SECRETARY FASCIST PARTY

SECRETARIES OF PROVINCIAL PARTY ORGANIZATIONS

SECRETARIES OF LOCAL PARTY ORGANIZATIONS

THE GOVERNMENT

HEAD OF GOVERNMENT MUSSOLINI

COUNCIL OF MINISTERS

COURTS AND TRIBUNALS

CHAMBER OF FASCI AND CORPORATIONS

THE SENATE — APPOINTED FOR LIFE

PREFECTS OF PROVINCES

PODESTA OF LOCAL GOVERNMENTS

government, is selected by the Duce and approved by
the King; from three to eight of these posts are commonly held by Mussolini himself. Most strategic among
governing bodies is the Grand Council, directorate of
the Fascist Party, of which Mussolini is president and
whose members are chosen by him. Upon the Grand
Council devolves the duties of assisting the Duce upon
matters of government, co-ordinating Party activities,
appointing provincial officials, and (in effect) selecting
Mussolini's successor.

Fascist legislation appears in the form of decrees
issued by the head of the government or of measures
formulated in conjunction with the ministers and the
Grand Council. The Italian parliament consists of
two houses, a senate whose members are appointed for
life, and the newly inaugurated Chamber of Fasci and
Corporations. The latter replaced the residual Chamber of Deputies, which had been elected under a qualified suffrage. The new Chamber consists of appointive
officials selected from the Fascist Party, the National
Council of Corporations, and the employer and employee confederations—thus providing a degree of functional representation. Neither house initiates legislation, but both are empowered to approve certain cate-
gories of measures presented to them.

In general, the government is highly centralized at
Rome, with appointed officials administering national
policy in the communities and provinces. The judicial
system is consolidated under a minister of justice and,
like the legislative branch, provides no check upon the
executive power.

THE CORPORATIVE SYSTEM

The fascist economy represents a compromise between private capitalism and the requirements of the totalitarian state.[4] In its basic law, fascism approves the principles of private ownership and production, but immediately stipulates that the economy must be co-ordinated within the state program. Private enterprise is encouraged and protected, but its operation is bound up in a network of restrictions and regulations. The government may, at its discretion, expand or limit production, set wages, fix prices, define conditions of employment and dismissal, authorize or prevent new undertakings, subsidize existing enterprises, or operate its own. In such fields as credit, shipping, mining, and the production of war materials, private ownership has been supplanted by the state. Although the profit-motive remains as the incentive to production, the right of enterprisers to make independent decisions—a vital feature of capitalism—is severely curtailed.

True to its totalitarian concept, the fascist state refuses to sanction the existence of opposed economic or class interests. Industrial disputes in the form of strikes or lockouts are expressly forbidden. In a Charter of Labor, published in 1927, the state seeks to enforce the collaboration of employers and workers by fixing the status of both within a legal framework, with the government installed as final arbitrator. The conduct

---

[4] Mussolini has repeatedly declared that the survival of modern capitalism is possible only when its processes are given systematic direction by a superior body.

of his enterprise is left with the owner; workers must co-operate with management in the problems of production. Complaints by either group are subject to conciliation or settlement in labor courts, presided over by fascist officials.

In place of independent unions and trade associations, a corporative system, closely linked with the government, has been devised. Two main structures may be distinguished. First, there is a series of industrial councils in which employers and employees are organized separately, by industries. Local associations (syndicates) of each group are represented in regional federations, and these again in national confederations. The major task of these bodies is to prepare and administer collective labor contracts for their branches of industry. Such contracts are usually drafted to apply to a large area or to the whole nation.

In addition to this structure, the major industries of the nation are organized into twenty-two "corporations," under direct governmental control. Councils for each of the corporations are made up of members representing employers, employees, and the Fascist Party. All processes of economic activity—production, distribution, banking, labor relations, foreign trade, etc.—are supervised by a ministry of corporations, a department of the national government.

The entire corporative system is under Fascist Party control. Except in the syndical associations, where a measure of self-government prevails, officials are directly appointed by the government. It is in this control that the supremacy of the state over economic life is actually achieved.

SOCIAL SECURITY

Social-security provisions are administered in part by the government, the rest by mutual societies. Unemployment insurance, on a contributory basis, is compulsory for lower-grade workers. A broad program of public works has been carried on for some years to reclaim marshland, construct roads, and provide other improvements. In accordance with a policy of population increase, special benefits are granted for large families in the form of maternal welfare, bonuses, and tax reductions.

The *Dopolavoro* is an organization for recreational and cultural advancement of workers. It is administered by the Fascist Party and supported with funds contributed by members, syndicates, and public agencies.

FASCIST EDUCATION

The essential purpose of the educational system is to instil in Italian youth a devotion to the principles of fascism. The curriculum accordingly stresses the virtues of courage, duty, and discipline as superior to the search for objective knowledge. A large share of the educational program is devoted to military and physical training. Students are enrolled in semimilitary groups from the age of four upward, and it is from these that members of the Fascist Party and national militia are recruited.

As in the case of the Soviet Union, public instruction of all types is basically propagandist. The press, radio, stage, and screen are all enlisted in the same undertaking—that of molding public opinion for the furtherance of national aims.

FASCISM AND RELIGION

Religious affiliation in Italy is more than 99 per cent Roman Catholic, yet fundamental conflicts lie at the base of relations between fascism and the church. In its very nature, totalitarianism precludes the sharing of allegiance with another. Moreover, in stressing the worth of human personality, the church clashes directly with the fascist insistence on its own morality, in which the individual is submerged in the collective scheme.

As a result of the Lateran Accord of 1929, these differences have been temporarily abated. Religious instruction is now a part of the public-school curriculum, but the training of youth remains exclusively in state hands. No religious organization may exercise functions performed by the state or external to its purposes.

By a series of anti-Semitic decrees issued in 1938, Jews were placed under various disabilities and a large number expelled from the country.

FASCISM *vs.* DEMOCRACY AND LIBERALISM

The postwar turmoil that marked the end of Italy's experience with popular government contributed largely to the nation's acceptance of an authoritarian regime. To this same experience, brief but unfavorable, may be traced fascism's relentless opposition to every element of the liberal-democratic faith.

The fascist state rejects completely the basic assumptions of democracy—that all men deserve equality of status, that the masses of the people have the right to choose their rulers, that the interplay of public opinion is desirable, and that the powers of government rest on popular consent. As opposed to these principles, fascism affirms the "permanent and fruitful inequality" of classes and the right of a self-appointed elite to rule. It makes no pretense of utilizing universal suffrage; and in place of the unwieldy parliamentary system with its crosscurrents of public opinion, it prefers a political structure whose keystone is absolute authority, "quick, sure, unanimous."

In the sphere of individual freedom this contrast is most acute. In fascist theory, freedom is a monopoly of the state and may be exercised by individuals only for state purposes. To put it otherwise: freedom, instead of being an inherent right of the individual (as liberals would have it), is a qualified grant by the state, for the period of good behavior. Fascists maintain that, since the state speaks for a unified people, opposition to its will is a criminal offense and not to be tolerated.

The center of reference is at all times the welfare of the state, to which other interests must be subordinate. Contrary to the liberal notion, fascism declares that the individual exists for the state, not the state for the individual. As an isolated unit, man is held to be without meaning; it is only when he becomes a part of the collective whole that he becomes significant.

An additional contrast may be noted. The liberal-democratic tradition is an appeal to the rational and logical in experience; that of fascism, to the emotional and mystical. Fascists claim for their doctrine a spiritual base, as opposed to the "gross materialism" of the western democracies.

It should be noted as well that fascism does not feel itself bound by requirements of consistency in furthering its program. It is interested in ends alone, not means, and the state reserves the right to use whatever methods may be effective in the circumstances.[5]

FASCISM vs. SOCIALISM

In spite of an evident similarity in the ordering of collective life, fascism is no less opposed to socialism, which, in fact, it stigmatizes as the logical outcome of democracy. In contrast to the economic well-being aimed at by socialists, fascism emphasizes the heroic virtues of discipline and sacrifice. The role of economic forces in shaping society is challenged as an exaggeration; particularly the Marxian doctrine of the class struggle. To the fascist, the state is not what Marx claimed—an instrument of class domination—but rather the highest expression of national unity. Instead of "withering away," the state is expected ultimately to include the totality of existence.

In contrast to the proposal for public ownership of

---

[5] Unlike the example of the Soviet Union, the Italian regime is not the achievement of a preformulated doctrine. The main part of fascist theory, even the conception of the state, was devised after Mussolini's accession to power in 1922.

production, fascism prefers private ownership under state guidance. Where socialists preach internationalism, fascist loyalties stop at the national borders.

Italian fascism originated as the opposition to the socialization movement in Italy during the postwar years and was successful in stamping out the "left-wing" parties.

FOREIGN POLICY

An intense spirit of nationalism and a passion for imperial greatness pervade the fascist world outlook. Nations are regarded as exclusive competitive units, urged on by motives of self-interest. It is inconceivable to fascism that any existing international status should be accepted as permanent, or that a strong nation will forego expansion out of regard for weaker neighbors.

Perpetual peace is rejected as neither desirable nor possible. War is not only the eternal law of mankind but the true evidence of a nation's vitality. Yet fascism regards both peace and war in a pragmatic sense—not as matters of moral concern but as instruments of national policy. The state reserves the right to follow whatever course may, in the circumstances, promote its interests.

Institutions designed solely to maintain peace are ignored. The fascist state chooses to remain aloof, to shun international commitments, and to pursue its imperial destiny unchecked.

CHAPTER XIV

Nazism
(German Fascism)

NAZISM[1] is properly identified as the German version of fascism, but it contains a number of elements peculiar to its national setting.

BACKGROUND

Out of Germany's First World War defeat emerged the Weimar Republic, patterned in the shape of liberal democracy. Unlike the instance of Russia, the communist bid for power in Germany had failed, and the new government began its brief career with representative institutions, the separation of powers, and broad guarantees of individual freedom.

The Weimar Republic, under Social Democratic leadership, was notable as an attempt to invoke gradualistic methods to reach ultimate socialism. But the postwar problems of the new regime proved insurmountable. Reformist legislation clashed with existing property interests, with monarchist survivals, and with religious conservatism; the government veered from Left to Right, satisfying neither group and alienating both. In spite of considerable foreign aid, the nation staggered under the burden of postwar reconstruction, a

[1] Derived from the name *Nationalsozialistische Deutsche Arbeiterpartei* (National Socialist German Labor Party).

condition aggravated by the loss of its vital resources. Over the whole experiment hung the oppressive atmosphere of defeatism, of which the Versailles Treaty was the bitter symbol. With German industry operating on "borrowed prosperity," the onset of the world-wide depression in 1929 shattered whatever hope remained of recovery. The temper of the nation no longer permitted moderate reform. A radical transference of political power was unavoidable.

In the ensuing struggle for dominance, the National Socialist German Labor Party of Adolf Hitler crushed the opposition of the Left and was elevated to power in the early months of 1933.[2] An Enabling Act, passed March 24, 1933, granted the national cabinet the right to enact laws without consent of the German parliament. Following the death of the Reich president, von Hindenburg, soon after, the post of president was combined with that of chancellor and both vested in the person of Adolf Hitler. Opposition parties were quickly outlawed, personal liberties abolished, and the nation reorganized under authoritarian rule.

THE TOTALITARIAN STATE

Like Italy, the Nazi state is a totalitarian unit. Every phase of the individual and collective life is "co-ordinated" within a single scheme, animated by a single

---

[2] National Socialist support came chiefly from the following broad groups: both large and small business enterprisers, the depressed middleclass and "white-collar" workers, dissatisfied farmers, and the youthful unemployed. The Nazi Party program was successful in channeling a variety of discontents, fears, and generalized yearnings into an organized opposition against the government and the proletarian parties.

purpose, and subjected to a single will—that of the *Fuehrer* (leader). In the government, authority is imposed from the top, with obedience acknowledged from below. Economic interests are subordinated to political ends. Public opinion is shaped in the official mold, and even the findings of science must conform to approved doctrine. The state as an organic unity stands above all institutions within it and besides this carries the timeless destiny of the German people.

THE LEADER PRINCIPLE AND THE NAZI PARTY

Control of the entire social structure is effected through the "leadership principle." The leaders, exclusively members of the Nazi Party, constitute a small, select ruling class, responsible only to their superiors. All others, in every function of national life, are followers, from whom loyalty and obedience are expected. All are to be trained in the principles of National Socialism; the most promising candidates will become members of the Party; and from among these are selected the leaders of the state.

The processes of governing are a monopoly of the leader class, responding to the will of the supreme Fuehrer. A complex administrative machine, reaching into every function of the national life, is maintained by the Nazi Party. Constituent bodies, such as the uniformed Storm Troopers and Elite Guards, together with affiliated groups of a professional and occupational nature, enforce the co-ordination program of the Party in their respective fields. Authority extends, in all cases, from above; obedience flows upward.

The Government of Nazi Germany

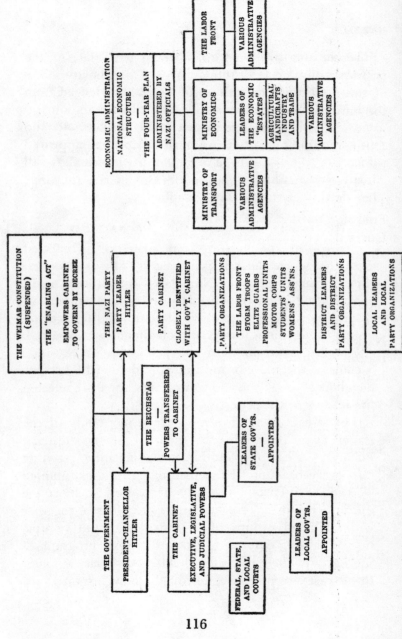

The Nazi Party must be regarded as more than a mere political body. It is an integral part of the state, bearer of the Germanic tradition, and the axis about which the national life revolves.

The structure of government is highly centralized. Ultimate power of decision rests with the supreme leader and is delegated through Nazi Party channels to every administrative position. (See chart on page 116.) Laws are issued in the form of decrees by the Fuehrer, through the instrumentality of his cabinet. Government is by executive and administrative order alone; no legislative or judicial check exists. The various political subdivisions, provinces and municipalities, are administered by officials appointed by, and responsible to, the national government.

A revised judicial system, in which the principles of National Socialism have been applied to the administration of justice, has been established on a uniform basis for the courts of the nation.

ECONOMIC ORGANIZATION

The word "Socialism" as a part of the name "National Socialism" is misleading. A more accurate designation of both the Italian and German economies would be "State Capitalism"[3]—indicating privately owned, profit-motivated enterprise operating under rigid state control.

The dominant feature of the German economy is the strict supervision of every process by state agencies. Although industry remains for the most part in private

---

[3] See the definition of this term in Chap. IV.

hands, its conduct is shaped by the prior demands of national welfare. Over all branches of enterprise is set the administrative structure of the Nazi Party, through which co-ordination of policy and satisfaction of performance are secured.

But within this official framework there prevails an economic version of the leadership principle. The owner or manager of an enterprise is designated as the leader, with his employees classified as followers. Both are expected to discharge their respective duties faithfully and to submerge their conflicting demands in the national interest. Upon the businessman as leader rests the proper conduct of his enterprise. Within established limits he determines the use of his capital, the schedule of wages and hours of work, conditions of employment, rules of discipline, etc. Employers' associations in the various industries co-operate to achieve uniformity of production and labor policies.

The most fundamental change has occurred in the status of labor. Independent trade-union organizations are illegal, the procedure of collective bargaining has been eliminated, and strikes (or lockouts) are forbidden. Workers and employers alike are enrolled in an all-inclusive Labor Front under the administration of the Nazi Party. The purpose of the Labor Front is to neutralize the conflicting claims of capital and labor and to divert the struggle of workers for economic improvements into channels of cultural and recreational activity. A limited check upon the powers of the employer-leader is afforded by a system of labor trustees, shop councils, and courts of honor, in which the settlement of disputes is guided by the primacy of state interests.

The state reserves the right at all times to intervene in economic matters where issues of national concern are at stake. With this important proviso, National Socialism professes its full confidence in the adequacy of private enterprise. The amount of state ownership of industry is not unduly great; but the requirements of military policy and the struggle for national self-sufficiency have greatly expanded the scope of governmental control.

It should be recalled that long before the National Socialist regime came to power the German economy had reached a high degree of industrial concentration, exhibiting an abundance of monopolies and corporate combinations, both public and private. The Nazis have fitted this framework into the totalitarian scheme, depriving labor of its independent role, elevating the employer to the status of industrial leader, and making both strictly accountable to the state.

DOCTRINE OF RACIAL SUPREMACY

The center of gravity of the National Socialist creed lies in the doctrine of German racial supremacy. A new "race science" has been evolved, from which the following conclusions are derived:

1. Mankind is divided into several grades of superior (pure) and inferior (mixed) races.

2. Among all these the Germanic (Nordic, Aryan) race occupies the highest level.

3. The physical and cultural attributes of racial groups

are fixed for all their members by heredity and can be improved or debased only through intermarriage—the effect
of environmental factors, in other words, is strictly limited.

The fact of race, Nazis maintain, has determined the
shape of human development; and it is claimed that
whatever major accomplishments can be discerned in
world history are traceable to Germanic efforts.

The implications of this doctrine are profound and
far-reaching. As carriers of a superior civilization, the
Germanic race feels itself justified in imposing its will
upon lesser peoples by whatever means it may choose.
Racial supremacy acknowledges no morality or law
higher than its own: every act that is "German" is
automatically justified.

In the official program of anti-Semitism this doctrine
finds its most severe application. Jews are denounced
as the most degenerate of races and the apostles of all
that Nazism despises: pacifism, internationalism, Christianity, social equalitarianism, communism, international finance, personal freedom, the notion of human
brotherhood, etc. From these contaminating influences
National Socialism has succeeded in rescuing Aryan
culture. A policy of "economic eradication" of the
Jews has been pursued by the government. Their personal and civil rights have been abolished, and segregation into ghettos has been decreed for those who remain
in the country.

EDUCATION, SCIENCE, AND PROPAGANDA

National Socialism rejects without qualification the
moral and ethical values of liberal democracy. In place

of these, it professes a new ideology based upon racial exclusiveness and the claims of totalitarian life. Education, science, and propaganda lose their distinctions and are fused into a single instrument of national policy, permeating the entire social structure. Public schools, universities, the press, the radio, and the theater are wholly in the service of the state and take their impulses from political needs. Truth is declared to be an aspect of "race," an intuition of superior "blood" rather than of objective knowledge.

Consistent with the declaration, "who has the youth holds the future of Germany," the state assumes the task of training the child from his earliest years and of molding his behavior throughout adulthood. Boys and girls are enrolled in Hitler Youth groups at the age of ten; primary stress is laid on sports, military training, and the mastery of National Socialist principles. The public-school curriculum continues this emphasis throughout the years of adolescence. Through the medium of the National Socialist Teachers' League, in which instructors of all grades are enrolled, systematic uniformity in education is assured.

The Ministry of Public Enlightenment and Propaganda, under the direction of Dr. Goebbels, wields broad powers of control over newspapers, literature, radio, theater, and cultural arts, co-ordinating their functions with the requirements of the state.

FOREIGN POLICY

The implications of Germanic racial supremacy are reflected in an aggressive and expansionist foreign policy. The German ."master race," it is maintained, is inherently destined to rule over others by virtue of its superiority. The natural state of peoples is affirmed to be that of warfare; pacifism is a sign of national decadence, and peace associations a conspiracy of the weak to undermine the strong. War is exalted as the supreme expression of national greatness, its use as an instrument being guided solely by the demands of the state. Totalitarian warfare reaches its highest refinement in the complete mobilization of the nation's military, economic, and psychological forces.

In response to this dynamic outlook, the character of the German state is that of a disciplined military unit. The scope of German influence is declared to be universal, and the conquest of other peoples, whether by force or coercion, is intended to produce an aggregation of subject states designed to minister to the needs of the National Socialist superstate.

As a corollary to the doctrine of the German blood bond, it is insisted that loyalty to the Fatherland must transcend the allegiance of Germans to any other state in which they may reside.

CHAPTER XV

Consumers' Co-operation
(The Co-operative Movement)

THE CO-OPERATIVE MOVEMENT is the name used to
describe several forms of voluntary activity by
which organized groups own and operate business enterprises for the mutual benefit of their members. The most typical form of this activity is known
as consumers' co-operation, to which the major part of
this description is devoted. Other forms of co-operation
are briefly defined.

ATTITUDE TOWARD CAPITALISM

Consumers' co-operation springs from a basic concern for the welfare of the consumer in the economic
scheme. The contention is made that, no matter what
the form of economy may be, there is only one group
that is universal, only one function in which all share
equally—that of the consumer. The satisfaction of the
consumer ought therefore to be the guidepost for the
furnishing of economic goods and services.

As now constituted, business enterprisers, investors,
and workers each pursue their own narrow group interests, in competition or sometimes even in collusion with
each other; regardless whose advantage is immediately
served, the consumer pays the bill. The good of all
becomes a sacrifice to the greed of selfish interests.

Co-operators contend that in a capitalist economy consumers have become the victims of the profit motive. When the output of goods and services is controlled solely by the prospect of personal gain, a number of serious abuses become evident: monopolistic practices, excessive costs, competitive wastes, needless duplication, fraudulent advertising, adulteration and misbranding of goods, diversion of capital to the field of luxury goods, and the like. As a result, concern for the consumer as such is no more than a casual by-product of the search for profits.

Co-operators have no quarrel with the other institutions of capitalism. The right of free enterprise, the wage system, the competitive market, private property —these are no less a feature of co-operation than of capitalism.

HOW CO-OPERATIVES FUNCTION

To ensure their own welfare, then, co-operative societies consisting of a group of organized consumers, arrange to set up business enterprises in competition with private concerns. The enterprise might take the form of a retail market, cafeteria, service station, clothing store, or similar venture. Capital to finance the venture is obtained by the sale of shares to members, ordinarily in five- or ten-dollar denominations. The society entrusts the management of the business to an elected board of directors, which hires the necessary employees and is responsible for general policy. In a retail store, two kinds of goods are sold: (1) standard products obtained through normal trade channels; and

(2) co-operative brand products supplied by co-operative producing units. The latter are usually preferred whenever available. Directly or indirectly the members of each society can prescribe their own standards of quality and the conditions under which their business shall be run.

At regular meetings of the society, the net earnings of the enterprise are distributed. Generally, the fund is divided along these lines: (1) A small portion is set aside for educational and recreational activities. (2) A larger share is made available for expansion and improvement of the business. (3) The balance is apportioned in the form of rebates to members of the society on the basis of their purchases during the period.

Frequently such ventures as described above begin in a modest way, as "buying clubs," without an established place of business and with no paid employees. Capital obtained through payment of membership shares is augmented by refunds to the co-operative for business entered into by contracts with private firms. At least in its beginning stages, every co-operative depends to some degree upon the unpaid voluntary help of its members.

VERTICAL EXPANSION

The growth of consumers' co-operatives does not halt with the establishment of a retail-store outlet. The next advance comes with the formation of a wholesale distributive center by several retail societies, which administer and control the larger unit. As opportunity offers, wholesaling moves on to importing, warehousing, processing, and manufacturing. At each step the profits ordinarily reserved to private enterprisers are made available to the member societies financing the operations and are again apportioned on the basis of patronage. In its ultimate form, co-operative enterprise foresees a complete nonprofit cycle from the extraction of raw materials to the distribution of finished consumers' goods.

UNDERLYING PRINCIPLES

Consumers' co-operatives agree upon several principles as providing a common basis for the conduct of their societies and business affairs. Most of these derive from the rules laid down by the Rochdale Equitable Pioneers' Society, established in England in 1844. The following principles generally identify the "true" co-operative:

1. Membership in a society is open to all, without discrimination as to race, creed, color, sex, or political affiliation.

2. Affairs of the society are conducted on a democratic basis, with an elected board of directors to serve in an executive capacity. Regular meetings are held, open to all members.

3. Each member is entitled to but one vote in the conduct of the society, no matter how many shares of capital he may hold. Voting by proxy is not permitted.

4. The investment capital raised by the sale of membership shares represents a loan, usually earns a low fixed rate of interest, and is returnable on termination of membership.

5. Net earnings of the business are refunded to members,

not on the basis of shareholdings, but on the proportionate amount of purchases made.

6. Business is conducted as far as possible for cash. Goods are customarily sold at current market prices, except in such cases as the co-operative feels it may safely undersell private competitors.

7. Goods and services may be sold to the public at large, but only members receive patronage refunds. (Frequently, purchases of nonmembers are credited toward payment of membership shares.)

8. Societies usually maintain a neutral position with regard to religious, political, or other controversial matters.

9. Employees of co-operative enterprises are encouraged to organize into trade unions for purposes of collective bargaining. Co-operative employees are often members of the society for which they work.

10. Societies co-operate with each other on a district or regional basis for purposes of business, education, publicity, or expansion of activities.

TYPES OF CO-OPERATIVES

Four main types of co-operative societies may be distinguished.

The first and "truest" type is the *consumers' co-operative* described above. It aims to supply its members with an adequate amount of goods or services of assured quality at low prices. Ventures in this field include retail stores vending such articles as groceries, meats, dairy products, drugs, clothing, gasoline, and oil; service associations for housing, insurance, medical care, hospitals, laundries, cafeterias; the supplying of gas, heat, water, and electricity; and a variety of other economic and social services ordinarily operated as profit-making businesses. Sometimes, as in the case of bakeries and creameries, the societies function in both production and distribution. It will be recalled that, whenever feasible, these activities expand into the wholesaling, processing, and manufacturing fields.

Credit co-operatives, better known as credit unions, serve their members (1) as deposit and savings banks; (2) as a source of loans at low interest; and (3) as an agency of education in business practices. In the United States credit unions operate under special legislation. Each society is usually restricted to the membership of some large industrial firm, labor union, government agency, church, or other organized group.

Marketing co-operatives are the societies organized chiefly by ranchers and farmers for the purpose of collaborating in the growing, shipping, and marketing of their products. These co-operatives flourish among vegetable, fruit, grain, cotton, and tobacco growers, among dairy and poultry producers, and among livestock-shipping associations. Frequently, such societies are converted into general, all-purpose co-operatives that buy, produce, and sell on a collective basis.

Producers' co-operatives are associations either of industrial workers or of farmers who pool their skills and resources, produce goods for sale, and share the income on some agreed basis. Producers' co-operatives are to be found in farming communities, coal mines, canneries, cigar factories, and the like, but are still somewhat rare in this country. Except when functioning in connection with consumer groups, these are not considered "true" co-operatives, since their emphasis is on profit-sharing production rather than on service to the consumer.

Self-help co-operatives, a special outgrowth of depression years, are associations of the unemployed that, by means of barter, salvage, and small-scale production activities, derive an income which is distributed among the members in the form of cash, commodities, or services.

EXTENT OF THE MOVEMENT

The co-operative movement is world-wide in scope, embracing a total membership of approximately 100,-000,000 persons, who belong to some 300,000 co-operative societies of all types. Of these, the great bulk are consumers' groups. The above figures do not include the impressive totals of the Soviet Union, where the close integration of co-operative societies with the socialized economy makes their function essentially different from those operating elsewhere. In the United States, co-operatives have shown a substantial growth but still represent only a small percentage of total economic activity. The number of societies of all types exceeds 20,000; membership is in the neighborhood of 5,000,000.

In most countries, co-operative associations serve to unify the programs and objectives of member societies on a geographical or functional basis. The International Co-operative Alliance, with headquarters in London, is a federation of national societies representing some forty-one countries. The co-operative movement has been developed most extensively in Great Britain,

Switzerland, Norway, Sweden, Denmark, Finland, Mexico, and the Soviet Union.

TWO VIEWS OF THE CO-OPERATIVE MOVEMENT

Two main points of view persist with regard to the long-range aims of the co-operative movement. The more conservative co-operators are content to keep their movement permanently within the boundaries of capitalism. Their objectives begin and end with the effort to improve the standard of living, especially among low-income groups. According to this point of view, co-operatives are ready to enter only those fields in which distribution costs are excessive, where private business is unwilling to assume the risk, or where competition is needed to curb monopoly.

The second view is more ambitious. It foresees the eventual realization of a "co-operative commonwealth" in which nonprofit enterprise will have gradually supplanted private business in every field, from the extraction of raw materials to the sale of finished goods. Government ownership would in this case be extended to such projects as transportation, communication, and power production, which are not amenable to co-operative control. In such a society, the motivation of economic activity would be shifted from the quest for profits to the satisfying of needs. And in such an atmosphere, it is believed, there would exist more harmonious relationships. Economic co-operation would breed social harmony, just as private gain breeds exploitation. The principles of democracy could under such circumstances be more fully realized than heretofore possible. In this view, the end result of co-operation is not only a sounder economy but a better society.

The prospects of the co-operative movement appeal strongly to those who are convinced of the need for comprehensive social change, yet are unwilling to accept the methods and consequences of drastic action. But the likelihood of such a peaceful transition is denied by others who maintain that any serious displacement of private enterprise would promptly cause the destruction of the movement by those who control the processes of the capitalistic state.

Selected Readings

I. GENERAL WORKS

Americana Institute. *Isms.* N. Y., 1939.

Bryson, Lyman. *Which Way America? Communism, Fascism, Democracy.* Macmillan, N. Y., 1939.

Coker, Francis W. *Recent Political Thought.* Appleton-Century, N. Y., 1934.

Colton, Ethan T. *Four Patterns of Revolution.* Association Press, N. Y., 1935.

Columbia Encyclopedia: Articles under subject headings.

Counts, Villari, Rorty, and Baker. *Bolshevism, Fascism, and Capitalism.* Yale University Press, New Haven, 1932.

Davis, Jerome. *Contemporary Social Movements.* Appleton-Century, N. Y., 1930.

Encyclopedia Britannica: Articles under subject headings.

Encyclopedia of the Social Sciences: Articles under subject headings.

Foreign Policy Association. *Changing Governments.* N. Y., 1937.

Hoover, Calvin B. *Dictators and Democracies.* Macmillan, N. Y., 1937.

Joad, C. E. M. *Introduction to Modern Political Theory.* Clarendon Press, Oxford, 1924.

Laidler, Harry W. *A History of Socialist Thought.* Crowell, N. Y., 1927.

Law, L. E., and others. *Five Political Creeds—Fascism, Socialism, Communism, Liberalism, Conservatism.* Ryerson, Toronto, 1938.

Loucks, W. N., and Hoot, J. Weldon. *Comparative Economic Systems —Capitalism, Socialism, Communism, Fascism, Co-operation.* Harper, N. Y., 1938.

MacKenzie, Findlay (Editor). *Planned Society, Yesterday, Today, Tomorrow.* Prentice-Hall, N. Y., 1937.

Niebuhr, Reinhold. *Reflections on the End of an Era.* Scribner, N. Y., 1934.

Oakeshott, Michael J. *The Social and Political Doctrines of Contemporary Europe.* Cambridge University Press, Cambridge, 1939.

Page, Kirby (Editor). *A New Economic Order.* Harcourt, Brace, N. Y., 1930.

132

Parmelee, Maurice F. *Bolshevism, Fascism, and the Liberal-Democratic State.* Wiley, N. Y., 1934.

Russell, Bertrand. *Proposed Roads to Freedom.* Holt, N. Y., 1919.

Schmalhausen, Samuel D. (Editor). *Recovery Through Revolution.* Covici, Friede, N. Y., 1933.

Tracy, M. E. *Our Country, Our People, and Theirs.* Macmillan, N. Y., 1938.

Weisbord, Albert. *The Conquest of Power—Liberalism, Anarchism, Syndicalism, Socialism, Fascism, and Communism.* Covici, Friede, N. Y., 1937.

Westmeyer, Russell E. *Modern Economic and Social Systems.* Farrar & Rinehart, N. Y., 1940.

Zimand, Savel. *Modern Social Movements.* Wilson, N. Y., 1921.

II. ANARCHISM

Adamic, Louis. *Dynamite: The Story of Class Violence in America.* Viking, N. Y., 1934.

Baldwin, Roger N. (Editor). *Kropotkin's Revolutionary Pamphlets.* Vanguard, N. Y., 1927.

Berkman, Alexander. *Now and After, the ABC of Communist Anarchism.* Vanguard, N. Y., 1929.

Carr, Edward Hallett. *Michael Bakunin.* Macmillan, London, 1937.

David, Henry. *The History of the Haymarket Affair.* Farrar & Rinehart, N. Y., 1936.

Eltzbacher, Paul. *Anarchism.* Tucker, Boston, 1908.

Goldman, Emma. *Living My Life.* Knopf, N. Y. 1931.

————. *Anarchism and other Essays.* Mother Earth, N. Y., 1910.

Hunter, Robert. *Violence and the Labor Movement.* Macmillan, N. Y., 1914.

Kropotkin, Peter. *Memoirs of a Revolutionist.* Houghton, Mifflin, Boston, 1930.

————. *The Conquest of Bread.* Vanguard, N. Y., 1926.

————. *Mutual Aid.* Knopf, N. Y., 1921.

Parsons, Albert R. *Anarchism, Its Philosophy and Scientific Basis.* Chicago, 1887.

Plekhanov, Georgii. *Anarchism and Socialism.* Kerr, Chicago, 1918.

Reclus, Elisee. *An Anarchist on Anarchy.* Tucker, Boston, 1884.

Rocker, Rudolf. *Anarcho-Syndicalism.* Secker & Warburg, London, 1938.

Schuster, Eunice M. *Native American Anarchism.* Smith College Press, Northampton, 1932.

Shaw, George Bernard. *The Impossibilities of Anarchism.* Fabian Society, London, 1906.

Zenker, Ernest V. *Anarchism, a Criticism and History of Anarchist Theory.* Methuen, London, 1898.

III. CAPITALISM

Arnold, Thurman W. *The Folklore of Capitalism.* Yale University Press, New Haven, 1937.

Burns, Arthur R. *The Decline of Competition.* McGraw-Hill, N. Y., 1937.

Burns, Emile. *Capitalism, Communism, and the Transition.* V. Gollancz, London, 1933.

Commons, John R. *Legal Foundations of Capitalism.* Macmillan, N. Y., 1924.

Corey, Lewis. *The Decline of American Capitalism.* Covici, Friede, N. Y., 1934.

Cromwell, James H. R. *In Defense of Capitalism.* Scribner, N. Y., 1937.

Dahlberg, Arthur. *Jobs, Machines, and Capitalism.* Macmillan, N. Y., 1937.

Davis, Jerome. *Capitalism and Its Culture.* Farrar & Rinehart, N. Y., 1935.

Dobb, Maurice H. *Political Economy and Capitalism.* Routledge, London, 1937.

Edwards, George W. *The Evolution of Finance Capitalism.* Longmans, Green, N. Y., 1938.

Gras, Norman S. C. *Business and Capitalism.* Crofts, N. Y., 1939.

Johnsen, Julia E. (Compiler). *Capitalism on Trial.* Wilson, N. Y., 1931.

Newfang, Oscar. *Capitalism and Communism—a Reconciliation.* Putnam, N. Y., 1932.

Pigou, A. C. *Socialism vs. Capitalism.* Macmillan, N. Y., 1938.

Pitkin, Walter B. *Capitalism Carries On.* McGraw-Hill, N. Y., 1935.

Robbins, Lionel. *Economic Planning and International Order.* Macmillan, London, 1937.

Rogers, James Harvey. *Capitalism in Crisis.* Yale University Press, New Haven, 1938.

Smith, Adam. *The Wealth of Nations.* (Published in several editions.)

Snyder, Carl. *Capitalism the Creator.* Macmillan, N. Y., 1940.

Strachey, John. *The Nature of Capitalist Crisis.* Covici, Friede, N. Y., 1935.

Tawney, R. H. *Religion and the Rise of Capitalism.* J. Murray, London, 1926.

Veblen, Thorstein. *The Engineers and the Price System.* Modern Library, N. Y.

Withers, Hartley. *The Case for Capitalism.* Nash, London, 1920.

Wootton, Barbara. *Plan or No Plan.* Farrar & Rinehart, N. Y., 1935.

IV. CHRISTIAN SOCIALISM

Bennett, John C. *Christianity—and Our World.* Association Press, N. Y., 1936.

Campbell, Reginald John. *Christianity and the Social Order.* Macmillan, N. Y., 1907.

Dawson, Christopher H. *Religion and the Modern State.* Sheed & Ward, N. Y., 1935.

——————. *Beyond Politics.* Sheed & Ward, N. Y., 1939.

Dombrowski, James. *The Early Days of Christian Socialism in America.* Columbia University Press, N. Y., 1936.

Fellowship of Socialist Christians. *Christianity and Society* (quarterly publication), N. Y.

Figgis, J. N. *Churches in the Modern State.* Longmans, Green, N. Y., 1913.

Gladden, Washington. *Christianity and Socialism.* Jennings & Graham. Cincinnati, 1905.

Harris, H. W. (Editor). *Christianity and Communism.* Jones, Marshall, London, 1937.

Lewis, John (Editor). *Christianity and the Social Revolution.* Scribner, N. Y., 1936.

Luccock, H. E. *Christian Faith and Economic Change.* Abingdon, N. Y., 1906.

MacMurray, John. *The Clue to History.* Harper, N. Y., 1939.

Niebuhr, Reinhold. *Moral Man and Immoral Society.* Scribner, N. Y., 1932.

Nitti, F. S. *Catholic Socialism.* Macmillan, N. Y. 1908.

Noel, Conrad. *Socialism in Church History.* The Young Churchman Co., Milwaukee, 1911.

Plowright, Bernard C. *Rebel Religion.* Round Table, London, 1937.

Poteat, Edwin M. *The Social Manifesto of Jesus.* Harper, N. Y., 1937.

Rauschenbusch, Walter. *The Social Principles of Jesus.* Macmillan, N. Y., 1916.

Raven, Charles E. *Christian Socialism—1848-1854.* Macmillan, London, 1920.

Scott, R. B. Y., and Vlastos, Gregory (Editors). *Towards the Christian Revolution.* Gollancz, London, 1937.

Spargo, John. *The Spiritual Significance of Modern Socialism.* Viking, N. Y., 1908.

Vedder, Henry C. *Socialism and the Ethics of Jesus.* Macmillan, N. Y., 1912.

Ward, Harry F. *The New Social Order: Principles and Programs.* Macmillan, N. Y., 1920.

White, Bouck. *The Call of the Carpenter.* Doubleday, N. Y., 1914.

V. CO-OPERATIVE MOVEMENT

Alanne, V. S. *Fundamentals of Consumer Co-operation.* Northern States Co-operative League, Minneapolis, 1938.

Bakken, Henry H. *The Economics of Co-operative Marketing.* McGraw-Hill, N. Y., 1937.

Burley, Orin E. *The Consumers' Co-operative as a Distributive Agency.* McGraw-Hill, N. Y., 1939.

Carr-Saunders, A. M. *Consumers' Co-operation in Great Britain.* Allen & Unwin, London, 1938.

Childs, Marquis W. *Sweden, the Middle Way.* Yale University Press, New Haven, 1936.

Co-operative League of the U. S. *Yearbook.* N. Y.

Cowling, Ellis. *Co-operatives in America.* Coward-McCann, N. Y., 1938.

Daniels, John. *Co-operation, an American Way.* Covici, Friede, N. Y., 1938.

Fowler, Bertram B. *Consumer Co-operation in America.* Vanguard, N. Y., 1936.

Goslin, Ryllis A. *Co-operatives.* Foreign Policy Association, N. Y., 1937.

International Labor Office (League of Nations). *The Co-operative Movement and Better Nutrition.* Geneva, Switzerland, 1937.

Johnsen, Julia E. (Compiler). *Consumers' Co-operatives.* Wilson, N. Y., 1936.

Kallen, Horace M. *The Decline and Rise of the Consumer.* Appleton-Century, N. Y., 1936.

Lazo, Hector. *Retailer Co-operatives: How to Run Them.* Harper, N. Y., 1937.

May, Mark A., and Doob, Leonard V. *Competition and Co-operation.* Social Science Research Council, N. Y., 1937.

Mead, Margaret (Editor). *Co-operation and Competition Among Primitive Peoples.* McGraw-Hill, N. Y., 1937.

Neifeld, Morris R. *Co-operative Consumer Credit.* Harper, N. Y., 1936.

Panunzio, Constantine, Church, Wade, and Wasserman, Louis. *Self-Help Co-operatives in Los Angeles.* University of California Press, Berkeley, 1939.

Parker, Florence E. *Consumers' Credit and Productive Co-operation in 1933.* U. S. Government Printing Office, Washington, 1935.

Randall, Harlan J. *Consumers' Co-operative Adventures: Case Studies.* Whitewater Press, Whitewater, Wis., 1936.

Russell Sage Foundation. *Co-operative Housing.* N. Y., 1925.

U. S. Bureau of Labor Statistics. *Organization and Management of Consumers' Co-operative Associations and Clubs.* U. S. Government Printing Office, Washington, 1934.

U. S. Government Printing Office. *Report of the Inquiry on Co-operative Enterprise in Europe, 1937.* Washington, 1937.

Wallace, Henry A. *Co-operation: the Dominant Economic Idea of the Future.* 1936.

Warbasse, James P. *What Is Co-operation?* Vanguard, N. Y., 1927.

——————. *Co-operation as a Way of Peace.* Harper, N. Y., 1939.

——————. *Co-operative Democracy.* Macmillan, N. Y. 1927.

VI. DEMOCRACY

American Association for Adult Education. *Adult Education and Democracy.* N. Y., 1936.

Amidon, Beulah (Editor). *Democracy's Challenge to Education.* Farrar & Rinehart, N. Y., 1940.

Armstrong, Hamilton Fish. *We or They.* Macmillan, N. Y., 1937.

Arneson, Ben A. *The Democratic Monarchies of Scandinavia.* Van Nostrand, N. Y., 1939.

Ascoli, Max (Editor). *Political and Economic Democracy.* Norton, N. Y., 1937.

Barzun, Jacques. *Of Human Freedom.* Little, Brown, Boston, 1939.

Benes, Eduard. *Democracy Today and Tomorrow.* Macmillan, N. Y., 1939.

Berkson, Isaac B. *Theories of Americanization.* Teachers College, Columbia University, N. Y., 1920.

Bode, Boyd H. *Democracy as a Way of Life.* Macmillan, N. Y., 1937.

Bowers, Claude G. *Jefferson and Hamilton—the Struggle for Democracy in America.* Houghton, Mifflin, N. Y., 1926.

Brailsford, H. N. *Property or Peace.* Covici, Friede, N. Y., 1934.

Bryce, James. *Modern Democracies.* Macmillan, N. Y., 1927.

Carr, Robert Kenneth. *Democracy and the Supreme Court.* University of Oklahoma Press, Norman, 1934.

Clark, Gideon. *Democracy in the Dock.* Nelson, N. Y., 1940.

Counts, George S. *The Prospects of American Democracy.* John Day, N. Y., 1938.

Coyle, David Cushman, and others. *The American Way.* Harper, N. Y., 1938.

Everett, Samuel. *Democracy Faces the Future.* Columbia University Press, N. Y., 1935.

Gabriel, Ralph H. *The Course of American Democratic Thought.* Ronald, N. Y., 1940.

Gollomb, Joseph. *What's Democracy to You?* Macmillan, N. Y., 1940.

Hays, Arthur Garfield. *Democracy Works.* Random House, N. Y., 1939.

Institute of Human Relations, Williams College. *Public Opinion in a Democracy.* Princeton University Press, Princeton, 1938.

Laski, Harold J. *Democracy in Crisis.* University of North Carolina Press, Chapel Hill, 1933.

Lerner, Max. *It Is Later Than You Think.* Viking, N. Y., 1939.

Jones, F. Elwyn. *The Defense of Democracy.* Dutton, N. Y., 1938.

Lloyd, Christopher. *Democracy and Its Rivals.* Longmans, Green, N. Y., 1939.

McKinley, Silas B. *Democracy and Military Power.* Vanguard, N. Y., 1934.

Mann, Thomas. *The Coming Victory of Democracy.* Knopf, N. Y., 1938.

Martin, Everett Dean. *The Conflict of the Individual and the Mass in the Modern World.* Holt, N. Y., 1932.

Maverick, Maury. *In Blood and Ink.* Modern Age, N. Y., 1939.

Meiklejohn, Alexander. *What Does Democracy Mean?* Norton, N. Y., 1935.

Merriam, Charles E. *The New Democracy and the New Despotism.* McGraw-Hill, N. Y., 1939.

Muller, Helen Marie (Editor). *Democratic Collectivism.* Wilson, N. Y., 1935.

Newlon, Jesse H. *Education for Democracy in Our Time.* McGraw-Hill, N. Y., 1939.

Ohio State University. *Democracy in Transition.* Appleton-Century, N. Y., 1937.

Rappard, William E. *The Crisis of Democracy.* University of Chicago Press, 1938.

Rugg, Harold O. *Changing Governments and Changing Cultures.* Ginn, N. Y., 1937.

Smith, T. V. *The Democratic Way of Life.* University of Chicago Press, 1939.

Soule, George H. *An Economic Constitution for Democracy.* Yale University Press, New Haven, 1939.

Survey Graphic. *Calling America.* Harper, N. Y., 1939.

Tead, Ordway. *The Case for Democracy.* Association Press, N. Y., 1938.

Thomas, Wendell M. *A Democratic Philosophy.* Correlated Enterprises, N. Y., 1938.

Tocqueville, Alexis de. *Democracy in America.* Allyn, Boston, 1876.

Wilson, Milburn L. *Democracy Has Roots.* Carrick & Evans, N. Y., 1939.

VII. FABIANISM

Beer, Max. *History of British Socialism.* Macmillan, N. Y., 1919.

Cole, G. D. H. *The Machinery of Socialist Planning.* Hogarth Press, London, 1938.

Davies, Ernest. *How Much Compensation? A Problem of Transfer from Private to Public Enterprise.* Gollancz, London, 1937.

Fabian Society. *Where Stands Socialism Today?* Rich & Cowan, London, 1933.

Laidler, Harry W. *History of Socialist Thought.* Crowell, N. Y., 1927.

Pease, E. R. *History of the Fabian Society.* International, N. Y., 1926.

Shaw, George Bernard. *Essays in Fabian Socialism.* Constable, London, 1932.

VIII. FASCISM

Ashton, E. B. *The Fascist, His State, and His Mind.* Morrow, N. Y., 1937.

Borgese, G. A. *Goliath, the March of Fascism.* Viking, N. Y., 1938.

Dennis, Lawrence. *The Coming American Fascism.* Harper, N. Y., 1936.

Ebenstein, William. *Fascist Italy.* American, N. Y., 1939.

Finer, Herman. *Mussolini's Italy.* Holt, N. Y., 1936.

Florinsky, Michael T. *Fascism and National Socialism.* Macmillan, N. Y., 1936.

Fortune Magazine. Italian Number. July, 1934, N. Y.

Freeman, Ellis. *Conquering the Man in the Street.* Vanguard, N. Y., 1940.

Guerin, Daniel. *Fascism and Big Business.* Pioneer, N. Y., 1939.

Haider, Carmen. *Do We Want Fascism?* John Day, N. Y., 1934.

——————. *Capital and Labor Under Fascism.* Columbia University Press, N. Y., 1930.

Magil, A. B., and Stevens, Henry. *The Peril of Fascism.* International, N. Y., 1938.

Mussolini, Benito. *Fascism—Doctrines and Institutions.* Ardita, Rome, 1935.

Osbert, Reuben. *The Psychology of Reaction.* Gollancz, London, 1938.

Palmieri, Mario. *The Philosophy of Fascism.* Dante Alighieri Society, Chicago, 1936.

Rader, Melvin M. *No Compromise: the Conflict Between Two Worlds.* Macmillan, N. Y., 1939.

Raushenbush, Stephen. *The March of Fascism.* Yale University Press, New Haven, 1939.

Salvemini, Gaetano. *Under the Axe of Fascism.* Viking, N. Y., 1936.

Schmidt, Carl. *The Plough and the Sword.* Columbia University Press, N. Y., 1938.

Seldes, George. *You Can't Do That!* Modern Age, N. Y., 1938.

Steiner, H. Arthur. *Government in Fascist Italy.* McGraw-Hill, N. Y., 1938.

Strachey, John. *The Menace of Fascism.* Covici, Friede, N. Y., 1933.

Swing, Raymond Gram. *Forerunners of American Fascism.* Messner, N. Y., 1935.

IX. GUILD SOCIALISM

Carpenter, Giles. *Guild Socialism: an Historical and Critical Analysis.* Appleton-Century, N. Y., 1922.

Cole, G. D. H. *Self-Government in Industry.* Macmillan, N. Y., 1918.

——————— *Guild Socialism Restated.* Stokes, N. Y., 1921.

Field, Guy Cromwell. *Guild Socialism: a Critical Examination.* Gardner, Darton, London, 1920.

Hobson, S. G. *National Guilds and the State.* Bell, London, 1919.

Parkinson, Henry W. *From Capitalism to Freedom.* Labour Publishing Co., London, 1925.

Penty, Arthur J. *Guilds, Trade, and Agriculture.* Allen & Unwin, London, 1921.

Russell, Bertrand. *Proposed Roads to Freedom.* Holt, N. Y., 1919.

Taylor, G. R. S. *The Guild State, Its Principles and Possibilities.* Macmillan, N. Y., 1919.

Tawney, R. H. *The Acquisitive Society.* Harper, N. Y., 1920.

X. LIBERALISM

Chamberlain, John. *Farewell to Reform.* Liveright, N. Y., 1932.

Dewey, John. *Liberalism and Social Action.* Putnam, N. Y., 1935.

Hobhouse, Leonard T. *Liberalism.* Holt, N. Y., 1911.

Hobson, John A. *The Crisis of Liberalism.* King, London, 1909.

Hollander, Jacob H. *Economic Liberalism.* Abingdon, N. Y., 1925.

Hoover, Herbert C. *The Challenge to Liberty.* Scribner, N. Y., 1934.

Laski, Harold J. *The Rise of Liberalism—the Philosophy of a Business Civilization.* Harper, N. Y., 1936.

Lippmann, Walter. *The Good Society.* Little, Brown, N. Y., 1937.

Robertson, John M. *The Meaning of Liberalism.* Methuen, London, 1925.

Ruggiero, Guido de. *The History of European Liberalism.* Oxford University Press, London, 1927.

Schapiro, Jacob S. *Condorcet and the Rise of Liberalism.* Harcourt, Brace, N. Y., 1934.

Skinner, Clarence R. *Liberalism Faces the Future.* Macmillan, N. Y., 1937.

Smith, T. V. *The Promise of American Politics.* University of Chicago Press, 1936.

Soule, George. *The Future of Liberty.* Macmillan, N. Y., 1937.

Spender, Stephen. *Forward from Liberalism.* Random House, N. Y., 1937.

XI. MARXISM

Beer, Max. *A Guide to the Study of Marx.* 1923.

Brameld, Theodore. *A Philosophic Approach to Communism.* University of Chicago Press, Chicago, 1933.

Bukharin, N. I., and others. *Marxism and Modern Thought.* Harcourt, Brace, N. Y., 1935.

Burns, Emile (Editor). *Handbook of Marxism.* International, N. Y., 1935.

——————. *What Is Marxism?* Gollancz, London, 1939.

Cole, G. D. H. *What Marx Really Meant.* Knopf, N. Y., 1934.

Eastman, Max. *Marxism: Is It Science?* Norton, N. Y., 1941.

Engels, Friedrich. *Socialism, Utopian and Scientific.* International, N. Y., 1935.

Guest, David. *Dialectical Materialism.* International, N. Y., 1939.

Gurian, Waldemar. *The Rise and Decline of Marxism.* Burns, Oates & Washbourne, London, 1938.

Haldane, J. B. S. *The Marxist Philosophy and the Sciences.* Random House, N. Y., 1939.

Hook, Sidney. *Towards the Understanding of Karl Marx.* John Day, N. Y., 1931.

Jackson, T. A. *Dialectics, the Logic of Marxism.* Lawrence, London, 1936.

Laski, Harold J. *The State in Theory and Practice.* Viking, N. Y., 1935.

Lenin, V. I. *The Teachings of Karl Marx.* International, N. Y., 1933.

——————. *Marx-Engels-Marxism.* Lawrence, London, 1934.

——————. *What Is to Be Done?* Lawrence, London, 1934.

Levy, H. *A Philosophy for a Modern Man.* Knopf, N. Y., 1938.

Marx, Karl. *Capital, the Communist Manifesto, and Other Writings.* Modern Library, N. Y., 1932.

——————. *Selected Essays.* International, N. Y., 1926.

Mehring, Franz. *The Life of Karl Marx.* Covici, Friede, N. Y., 1936.

Murry, J. Middleton, and others. *Marxism.* Chapman & Hall, London, 1935.

Parkes, Henry Bamford. *Marxism, an Autopsy.* Houghton, Mifflin, Boston, 1939.

Postgate, Raymond W. *Karl Marx.* Hamilton, London, 1933.

Prenant, Marcel. *Biology and Marxism.* International, N. Y., 1938.

Russell, Bertrand, and others. *The Meaning of Marx.* Farrar & Rinehart, N. Y., 1934.

Selsam, Howard. *What Is Philosophy?* International, N. Y., 1939.

Strachey, John. *The Theory and Practice of Socialism.* Random House, N. Y., 1936.

——————————. *What Are We to Do?* Random House, N. Y., 1938.

Wolfe, Bertram D. *Marx and America.* John Day, N. Y., 1934.

XII. NAZISM

Abel, Theodore F. *Why Hitler Came to Power.* Prentice-Hall, N. Y., 1938.

American Council on Public Affairs. *Five Years of Hitler.* N. Y., 1938.

Ascoli, Max, and Feiler, Arthur. *Fascism for Whom?* Norton, N. Y., 1938.

Brady, Robert A. *The Spirit and Structure of German Fascism.* Viking, N. Y., 1937.

Childs, Harwood L. (Editor). *The Nazi Primer.* Harper, N. Y., 1938.

Drucker, Peter F. *The End of Economic Man.* John Day, N. Y., 1939.

Dutt, R. Palme. *Fascism and Social Revolution.* International, N. Y., 1935.

Ermarth, Fritz. *The New Germany.* Digest Press, Washington, 1936.

Hitler, Adolf. *Mein Kampf.* Reynal & Hitchcock, N. Y., 1939.

Kirkpatrick, Clifford. *Nazi Germany, Its Women and Family Life.* Bobbs-Merrill, N. Y., 1938.

Laurie, Arthur P. *The Case for Germany.* Internationaler Verlag, Berlin, 1939.

Lichtenberger, Henri. *The Third Reich.* Greystone, N. Y., 1937.

Marx, Fritz Morstein. *Government in the Third Reich.* McGraw-Hill, N. Y., 1937.

Rauschning, Hermann. *The Revolution of Nihilism.* Alliance, N. Y., 1939.

Reimann, Guenter. *The Vampire Economy.* Vanguard, N. Y., 1939.

Roberts, Stephen H. *The House That Hitler Built.* Harper, N. Y., 1938.

Schuman, Frederick L. *The Nazi Dictatorship.* Knopf, N. Y., 1935.

Snyder, Louis L. *From Bismarck to Hitler.* Bayard Press, Williamsport, Pa., 1935.

Stoddard, Lothrop. *Into the Darkness—Nazi Germany Today.* Duell, Sloan & Pearce, N. Y., 1940.

Warburg, Gustav Otto. *Six Years of Hitler—the Jews Under the Nazi Regime.* Allen & Unwin, London, 1939.

XIII. SOCIALISM

Dickinson, Henry D. *Economics of Socialism.* Oxford University Press, London, 1939.

Henderson, Fred. *The Case for Socialism.* Independent Labour Party, London, 1925.

Graves, Sally. *A History of Socialism.* Hogarth Press, London, 1939.

Laidler, Harry W. *American Socialism, Its Aims and Practical Program.* Harper, N. Y., 1937.

——————. *Socializing Our Democracy.* Harper, N. Y., 1935.

Man, Henri de. *The Psychology of Socialism.* Allen & Unwin, London, 1928.

Mises, Ludwig von. *Socialism, an Economic and Sociological Analysis.* Cape, London, 1936.

Page, Kirby. *Individualism and Socialism.* Farrar & Rinehart, N. Y., 1933.

——————. *Capitalism and Its Rivals.* Eddy & Page, N. Y., 1936.

Rappoport, Angelo S. *Dictionary of Socialism.* T. Fisher Unwin, London, 1924.

Shaw, George Bernard. *The Intelligent Woman's Guide to Socialism and Capitalism.* Brentano, N. Y., 1928.

Strachey, John. *The Nature of Capitalist Crisis.* Covici, Friede, N. Y., 1935.

Thomas, Norman M. *The Choice Before Us.* Macmillan, N. Y., 1934.

——————. *Socialism on the Defensive.* Harper, N. Y., 1938.

XIV. SOVIET COMMUNISM

Borkenau, Franz. *The Communist International.* Faber & Faber, London, 1938.

Browder, Earl. *What Is Communism?* Vanguard, N. Y., 1936.

——————. *The People's Front.* International, N. Y., 1938.

Chamberlain, William H. *Russia's Iron Age.* Little, Brown, N. Y., 1934.

Dimitrov, Georgi. *The United Front.* International, N. Y., 1938.

Eastman, Max. *Stalin's Russia and the Crisis in Socialism.* Norton, N. Y., 1940.

Florinsky, Michael T. *Toward an Understanding of the U.S.S.R.* Macmillan, N. Y., 1939.

Foster, William Z. *Toward Soviet America.* Coward-McCann, N. Y., 1932.

Gide, André. *Return from the U.S.S.R.* Knopf, N. Y., 1937.

Hecker, Julius F. *The Communist Answer to the World's Needs.* Chapman & Hall, London, 1935.

Hindus, Maurice. *The Great Offensive.* Smith & Haas, N. Y., 1933.

History of the Communist Party of the Soviet Union. International, N. Y., 1939.

Ilin, M. *New Russia's Primer.* Houghton, Mifflin, N. Y., 1931.

Johnson, Hewlett (Dean of Canterbury). *The Soviet Power.* International, N. Y., 1940.

Kerensky, Alexander. *The Crucifixion of Liberty.* John Day, N. Y., 1934.

Laski, Harold J. *Communism.* Holt, N. Y., 1932.

MacMurray, John. *The Philosophy of Communism.* Faber & Faber, London, 1933.

Sinclair, Upton, and Lyons, Eugene. *Terror in Russia?* R. R. Smith, N. Y., 1938.

Sloan, Pat. *Soviet Democracy.* Modern Age, N. Y., 1938.

Souvarine, Boris. *Stalin, a Critical Survey of Bolshevism.* Longmans, Green, N. Y., 1939.

Stalin, Josef. *Problems of Leninism.* International, N. Y., 1934.

Strachey, John. *The Theory and Practice of Socialism.* Random House, N. Y., 1936.

Strong, Anna Louise. *This Soviet World.* Holt, N. Y., 1936.

Vàrga, Eugene. *Two Systems, Socialist Economy and Capitalist Economy.* International, N. Y., 1939.

Ward, Harry F. *In Place of Profit.* Scribner, N. Y., 1933.

Webb, Sidney and Beatrice. *Soviet Communism, A New Civilization.* Scribner, N. Y., 1938.

Williams, Albert Rhys. *The Soviets.* Harcourt, Brace, N. Y., 1937.

Wolfe, Henry C. *The Imperial Soviets.* Doubleday, Doran, N. Y., 1940.

XV. STATE CAPITALISM (STATE SOCIALISM)

Adams, Arthur Barto. *National Economic Security.* University of Oklahoma Press, Norman, 1936.

American Academy of Political and Social Science. *Government Expansion in the Economic Sphere.* Philadelphia, ANNALS, v. 206, 1939.

——————. *Increasing Government Control in Economic Life.* ANNALS, v. 178, 1935.

Arnold, Thurman W. *The Bottlenecks of Business.* Reynal & Hitchcock, N. Y., 1940.

Beard, Charles A. (Editor). *America Faces the Future.* Houghton, Mifflin, Boston, 1932.

Bonn, Moritz J. *Economics and Politics.* Houghton, Mifflin, Boston, 1932.

Chase, Stuart. *Government in Business.* Macmillan, N. Y., 1935.

——————. *Idle Money, Idle Men.* Harcourt, Brace, N. Y., 1940.

Cheadle, John B. *No More Unemployed.* University of Oklahoma Press, Norman, 1934.

Douglas, Lewis W. *The Liberal Tradition; a Free People and a Free Economy.* Van Nostrand, N. Y., 1935.

Dykstra, Gerald O. *A Textbook on Government and Business.* Callaghan, Chicago, 1939.

Ezekiel, Mordecai. *Jobs for All Through Industrial Expansion.* Knopf, N. Y., 1939.

Frederick, J. George. *Readings in Economic Planning.* Business Bourse, N. Y., 1932.

Gaskill, Nelson B. *Profit and Social Security.* Harper, N. Y., 1935.

Greenwood, Ernest. *The Great Delusion.* Harper, N. Y., 1933.

Hall, Ford P. *Government and Business.* McGraw-Hill, N. Y., 1939.

Holcombe, Arthur N. *Government in a Planned Democracy.* Norton, N. Y., 1935.

Hurd, Archibald S. *State Socialism in Practice.* Allan, London, 1925.

International Industrial Relations Institute. *On Economic Planning.* Covici, Friede, N. Y., 1935.

Lawley, Francis Edmund. *The Growth of Collective Economy.* King, London, 1938.

Lippincott, Benjamin E. (Editor). *Government Control of the Economic Order.* University of Minnesota Press, Minneapolis, 1935.

Tugwell, Rexford G. *The Industrial Discipline and the Governmental Arts.* Columbia University Press, N. Y., 1933.

Walling, W., and Laidler, Harry W. *State Socialism, Pro and Con.* Holt, N. Y., 1917.

Young, Arthur Primrose. *Forward from Chaos.* Nisbet, London, 1933.

XVI. SYNDICALISM

Brissenden, Paul F. *History of the I.W.W.* Columbia University Press, N. Y., 1920.

Brooks, John Graham. *American Syndicalism: the I.W.W.* Macmillan, N. Y., 1913.

Cole, G. D. H. *The World of Labour.* Bell, London, 1933.

Dashar, M. *The Revolutionary Movement in Spain.* Libertarian Publishing Society, N. Y., 1935.

Elliott, William Y. *The Pragmatic Revolt in Politics.* Macmillan, N. Y., 1928.

Estey, James A. *Revolutionary Syndicalism.* King, London, 1913.

Harley, John H. *Syndicalism.* Dodge, N. Y., 1912.

Haywood, William. *Bill Haywood's Book.* International, N. Y., 1929.

Lewis, Arthur D. *Syndicalism and the General Strike.* Unwin, London, 1912.

Lorwin, Lewis L. *Syndicalism in France.* Columbia University Press, N. Y., 1914.

Pataud and Pouget. *Syndicalism and the Co-operative Commonwealth.* New International, Oxford, England, 1913.

Sorel, Georges. *Reflections on Violence.* Viking, N. Y., 1929.

Spargo, John. *Syndicalism, Industrial Unionism, and Socialism.* Viking, N. Y., 1913.

Tridon, Andre. *The New Unionism.* Viking, N. Y., 1913.